S0-DZO-079

The Little Self–Care Handbook

A Self-Love Kit for Women

GREGG MICHAELSEN

Copyright © 2020 Gregg Michaelsen and Confidence Builder LLC.

All rights reserved. No part of this publication may be reproduced, stored in a retrieval system, or transmitted in any form or by any means, electronic, mechanical, photocopying, recording, or otherwise, without written permission of the publisher.

DISCLAIMER: As a male dating coach I am very good at what I do because of my years of studying the nuances of interpersonal relationships. I have helped thousands of women understand men. That said, I am not a psychologist, doctor or licensed professional. So do not use my advice as a substitute if you need professional help.

Women tell me how much I have helped them and I truly hope that I can HELP you too in your pursuit of that extraordinary man! I will provide you with powerful tools. YOU need to bring me your willingness to listen and CHANGE!

Contents

The Little Self-Care Handbook

As you may or may not know, I receive and reply to emails from my readers every day. I love hearing from you and I genuinely want to help you. What became obvious to me over the past few years, is that you need a self-care kit. So, I worked with my team to create this beautiful self-care kit just for you!

Without further adieu, it is my pleasure to welcome you aboard the journey you are about to take. Before you begin, there are a few important things you should know:

1. Self-care isn't all about bubble-baths and glasses of wine; it's about taking care of all aspects of your life—physical, emotional, spiritual, intellectual, social and sensory

2. As you take this journey, what you will learn is life-changing

3. Not everything here will come easily to you—**that's okay!**

4. This journey has no end—it is a lifelong journey

5. While we must examine the negative to get to the positive, the focus of this journey is positivity, mindfulness and self-growth

6. It is not selfish to put time and effort into growing yourself; self-care is essential

7. There is no running time-clock; read and do these activities in your own time; some may be easy and can be done very quickly; others will be more challenging and may take days or weeks to complete; **that's okay!**

8. I am not a mental health professional; if you feel suicidal or extremely depressed, I strongly urge you to pause your work here and seek professional help first; you can return to this journal as you feel better

9. You are a beautiful person, inside and out; I firmly believe this; my goal is for you to believe it too!

10. You may print as many copies of the pages in the free downloadable workbook as you need but please do not share them with your friends; this is a copyrighted work, protected by the laws of copyright in the United States.

It is my goal to guide you through learning how to love who you are. It is **not** my goal to cause you any pain, however, going through some of these exercises and activities may cause you to relive some past pain. The only reason I ask you to do this is so you can heal and move forward in a healthy and happy way.

I just mentioned a free workbook. While most of the activities for the workbook are inside this book, it might be helpful to have the workbook so you can print the activities! Additionally, the workbook contains many journal pages, mentioned at the end of the book. Your first activity, just a page or so away, will be found in the workbook!

Download Free
Workbook and Journal at
**www.whoholdsthecardsnow.com/
free-self-care-workbook-sign-up/**

It's Nice to Meet Me

Please answer each question to the best of your ability at this time.

1. My full name is

2. I love

3. I am inspired by

4. A little thing that I can do to make a change in the world is

5. I am happiest when

6. I can't wait to

7. My happiest memory is

8. My favorite meal to cook is

9. I have never

10. I believe in

11. I love to listen to

12. I can't get enough of

13. A thing I often forget is

14. I am most thankful for

15. I feel prettiest when

16. I like to compliment others on

17. My best quality is

18. My favorite colors are

19. The most beautiful thing I have ever seen is

20. I hate

21. I can't stop thinking about

22. My favorite smell is

23. I am looking forward to

24. Something that might scare others that I don't find scary is

Self-Care General Information

Introduction

Before you take a deep-dive into self-care, I think it's important to let you know what's coming and help you prepare for this wonderful journey.

This book is divided into several sections. Six of those sections center on the six types of self-care, which you will learn about soon:

- Physical self-care
- Intellectual self-care
- Emotional self-care
- Social self-care
- Spiritual self-care
- Sensory self-care

Each of these types of self-care focuses on a different aspect of your life. No one type is more important than another and they all feed into one another to make a whole, healthy you.

My goal is to provide you with the tools you need to begin to grow your dating and relationship confidence. Before you can do so, you must develop the belief that you *can* improve your confidence.

Having high confidence before and after you enter a relationship prevents you from:

- Choosing a player, loser or narcissist

- Entering into a co-dependent relationship, which is always destined for failure

- Making your guy your hobby

Having high confidence also enables you to:

- Have a great story, therefore making you interesting to great men

- Maintain a healthy life outside of your relationship, which helps you remain mysterious and challenging to any great guy, something he craves

- Be naturally attractive to great men

As you proceed, you will develop your own goals and decide what is best for you and your future. Thank you for allowing me to be a part of your journey!

Six Areas of Self-Care

Self-care is often broken down into six life areas. Throughout this book, you will explore each of these six in a variety of ways.

Physical Self-Care

This is the most commonly recognized type of self-care. Physical self-care is about taking care of your body, but that doesn't only need to mean exercise. There are many other ways to take care of your body. Instead, I encourage you to make it about something you enjoy. If you aren't sure yet what that might be, please allow me to provide a few examples:

- Yoga
- Eating healthy meals
- Drinking more water
- Taking a walk
- Zumba
- Running
- Bike riding

Emotional Self-Care

This type of self-care enables you to get in tune with your emotions. This means checking in with yourself, uncovering your thought patterns, and becoming more mindful of triggers.

It also means learning how to work through those emotions, instead of avoiding or stuffing them down. In this type of self-care, you learn that it's okay to feel sad, hurt, angry, frustrated and happy. In cultivating emotional self-care, you are learning to have more compassion for yourself and your emotions. Some great examples of emotional self care are:

- Journaling
- Practicing mindfulness and meditation
- Setting boundaries
- Being creative

- Keeping a gratitude journal
- Working on changing negative self-talk and replacing it with positive self-talk

 ## Spiritual Self-Care

While this can be about religion, it doesn't need to be. This is about nourishing your spirit, your soul. With spiritual self-care, you develop a connection to something bigger than you to help you find meaning and purpose for your life. Doing this can provide you with the courage to push through when things get tough. It will help inspire hope over and over. A few great ways to practice spiritual self-care are:

- Meditation
- Spending time with nature
- Prayer
- Keeping a gratitude

journal
- Donating or volunteering for a charity or cause you believe strongly in

Intellectual Self-Care

This is the most often neglected type of self-care. When you're practicing intellectual self-care, you are nurturing and challenging your mind. To work in the area of intellectual self-care, you can determine what your strengths and talents are so you can nurture them further. It can also involve developing a new skill. Developing these areas of your life can help you determine a great career. Some great examples of intellectual self-care include:

- Reading a book

- Completing a puzzle

- Learning a new language

- Taking a course on something you're interested in

- Watching documentaries on topics that intrigue you

- Developing new hobbies

Social Self-Care

We are, by nature, social beings, but not everyone is comfortable in social settings. Even so, we still value connections to other people, even if the circle is small. Social self-care includes having a network of friends and family to lean on during tough times, trust with our deepest secrets and go to in order to celebrate the victories.

Some ways to practice social self-care are:

- Spending time with loved ones

- Having lunch with a friend

- Joining any type of class where you can make new friends who share your interests

- Reconnecting with an old friend

- Speaking to a stranger while you're waiting in line

Sensory Self-Care

This type of self-care is self-explanatory. This involves tweaking your senses and it's a very effective way to become mindful, something you will learn more about soon.

Some examples of sensory self care include: burning a scented candle, taking a warm bath, spending time in nature, listening to music you enjoy and walking barefoot in the grass.

Your Self-Care Preferences

Consider each of the types of self care you just learned about. Brainstorm a few ways in which you might want to practice self-care in each area. There is a workbook page for this activity.

Physical Self-Care

Intellectual Self-Care

Emotional Self-Care

Social Self-Care

Spiritual Self-Care

Sensory Self-Care

A Word on Mindfulness Before You Dive In

Much of what you will do in this journal is mindful, so you practice mindfulness in your life without realizing it. Being mindful, boiled down to its simplest terms, means being present in the current moment. If there are opposites to mindfulness, they are rumination and anxiety. Rumination means reworking the past, over and over. Anxiety is a fearful anticipation of something in the future. Then, it stands to reason that mindfulness is a great way to stop both of those harmful and negative behaviors.

My personal weakness is mindfulness. I've noticed this especially when I visit my elderly parents. I find myself in a rush to go somewhere I don't really need to be. My mind argues, "Gregg, there's something you need to do NOW." There wasn't.

What I've come to realize is that I drive away great moments, so I've worked hard to stop doing so. Now, I stay longer when visiting my family, even though it can become contentious. I recognize these are special moments and I'm learning to live in them instead of anxiously waiting for them to be over.

How do you practice mindfulness?

It's not that difficult to practice mindfulness. It simply means focusing on what is happening right now. For example, if you're reading this page and your thoughts are wandering back to something that happened earlier today or something you're worried about tomorrow, you aren't practicing mindfulness. You won't get much out of this activity.

Instead, refocus your thoughts to this page and only this page. Set those thoughts aside for another time. Just read these words and think about them.

The great news about practicing mindfulness is that you don't need to buy anything! All you need is to dedicate time and space to practice mindfulness.

Another piece of great news, especially if you've tried meditation but haven't been able to "quiet your mind," is that you don't need to quiet your mind in mindfulness. All you need to do is focus on the present.

Your mind will wander. This is the nature of being human. Learn to understand that your mind wandering isn't a bad thing, but you can control it. The art of being mindful is the art of recognizing that moment when your mind has drifted away from the present moment and bringing it back.

Another key aspect of being mindful is to learn to control the judgmental mind. While there are times when that internal critic may have saved you from a disaster, most of the time, it's not being helpful. Instead, learn to recognize those judgmental thoughts and diffuse them. How can you look at and react to the situation differently? When judgmental thoughts creep into your mindfulness practice, make a mental note of them and allow them to pass on by. Take a note of any sensations you feel when these judgments arrive and leave.

Mindfulness is about the continual practice of returning your mind to the here and now, regardless of which way it may wander or how many times.

To practice mindfulness, follow these steps:

1. Find a place to sit down. This place should make you feel calm and quiet.

2. Set a time limit, at least at first. Begin with just five to ten minutes and increase the time as you become better and more comfortable with it

3. Notice your body. Sit in a stable and comfortable position in which you can feel relaxed and calm.

4. Feel your breath. Take note of the sensation of breathing in and out; focus on that breathing

5. Take note of your wandering mind. When it does wander, return your attention to your breathing

6. Be kind to your mind as it wanders. Don't judge your thoughts or obsess over them. Simply allow them to flow through you as you return to your breathing.

If you have five minutes right now, why not give it a try. Write about your experience.

- How did it go?

- What thoughts tried to interfere in your mindfulness?

- Were you able to return to your breathing?

Don't be too hard on yourself. The first few times will be very challenging, especially when it comes to allowing judgmental thoughts to roll on by, but it'll become easier if you stick with it. Remember, it wasn't easy to write your name or ride a two-wheel bike the first time you did either of those, but now, you've mastered them both!

 ## A Special Note on Patience

Much of what you will be doing here requires patience with yourself. You might not be very good at that yet, but it's just like everything else and will come with practice. The workbook contains some wonderful 2" x 3" cards you can print out and keep close by. When you begin to feel frustrated or discouraged, pull out these cards!

Physical
Self-Care

Physical Self-Care

When you think about self-care, chances are you thought about physical self-care. It's the one most people are familiar with. In this section, you will focus on improving your physical self-care routine. On the following pages, you will:

- Determine what types of physical self-care appeal most to you

- Set physical self-care goals & rewards

- Set a physical self-care schedule you can stick to

- Evaluate your routine and make adjustments

- Learn how to overcome barriers to self-care

Pages in this section, each with a workbook page, include:

- Sleep tracker
- Goal worksheet
- Routine worksheet
- Weekly evaluation
- Barriers worksheet
- Physical self-care calendar
- Physical self-care ideas

One thing I want you to recognize about self-care is that it isn't meant to be full of things you hate doing. Yes, some of the workbook stuff you'll do here will make you feel a little uncomfortable, but in order to grow, you're going to feel a little discomfort from time to time. The trick is to begin to understand that the feeling of discomfort can come and go and leave you better for it.

Physical self-care is obviously about your physical being. It focuses on what you eat and drink, how you move your body and how well you take care of yourself with proper sleep and a balanced diet. I know it's not fun or sexy to think about eating more fruits and vegetables, but these healthy habits are important in maintaining a healthy body. Having said that, I'm not asking you to eat asparagus if you hate it.

I don't believe in elimination diets. Saying you'll *never* eat something again just makes you want it more. If you want a piece of chocolate cake, eat it, just don't eat three. If you want to go strictly vegan, go for it. Just make sure you're getting all the nutrients you need.

You know your body better than anyone else. You know how it responds to specific foods and which foods you should and shouldn't eat, so I'm not going to lecture you on what those foods are. You're an adult and you can figure it out on your own much better.

Taking care of your physical self also means getting enough sleep. Again, you know your body. Maybe you can get by on six hours, but it could also be that you need eight or nine. On the next page is a sleep tracker so you can begin to track this information and determine what truly is best for you. There is a copy of the sleep tracker in your free workbook.

The third aspect of physical self-care is moving your body. Notice I didn't say exercise. That word sparks a very negative response in some people, so instead, I want to encourage you to move your body. Take a few fifteen-minute walks during the day to refresh yourself. Find some two-pound weights and set them on your desk. When you have a few minutes or need to clear your head, do a few arm exercises. Put ankle weights on when you walk to improve the strength of your legs.

There are many ways in which you can move your body without calling it an exercise routine and they're all great. If you enjoy dancing, put on a video and dance your heart out every day after work. Whatever it is you decide to do, make it something you enjoy.

I do encourage you to try a Yoga class or Zumba. Go with a friend and give it a shot. Maybe a spin class is right for you or working with a trainer. Try a few things on for size and see what fits. If you end up with the walking routine, great. At least you were brave enough to try other things first.

If you're ready, let's get started! As you answer questions and complete the workbook pages, keep in mind that all you're working on right now is your physical self. We'll get to the other areas soon enough.

Finally, I encourage you to start with your physical self-care and work this into your routine for a week or so. Don't worry about trying to adopt all six types of self-care into your life at once. It is too overwhelming. Some of the activities you can incorporate cross over more than one type of self-care anyway and then, you're all set!

While self-care isn't something you need to do every day, I encourage you to take a different mindset with physical self-care. Having a healthy diet and moving your body are two things you should focus on daily.

On the next page is a visual of the sleep tracker included in the workbook. You can either create your own or use the one in the workbook! Your choice.

Sleep Tracker for (month) _____

Place a mark on each box for the hours during which you slept.

Date	Hour																							
	PM		AM											PM									
	10	11	12	1	2	3	4	5	6	7	8	9	10	11	12	1	2	3	4	5	6	7	8	9
1																								
2																								
3																								
4																								
5																								
6																								
7																								
8																								
9																								
10																								
11																								
12																								
13																								
14																								
15																								
16																								
17																								
18																								
19																								
20																								
21																								
22																								
23																								
24																								
25																								
26																								
27																								
28																								
29																								
30																								
31																								

Goals

It's great to have goals. Goals give you direction and provide focus where it might not feel as if you have any.

Accomplishing goals is also a great way to boost your confidence. The bigger the goal, the greater the boost to your confidence.

When you begin to think about setting goals, you may want to start by brainstorming some ideas of what you want out of your life in general.

Think ahead to one year from now. What does your life look like? Now, consider your life in three years. What does it look like?

Move your timeline out again, this time to five years. What does life in your world look like?

Take a plain piece of paper and do this brainstorming now. There isn't a workbook page for it because it's not meant to be a structured activity. Just write.

Get specific. Provide yourself with as many details as possible. For example, don't say you want to marry a great guy, Describe that guy in detail. What does he look like?

How tall is he? What color is his hair?

If you're describing the home you want to own some day, where is it? Suburbs or in a more urban setting? Is it a rural farmhouse? Is it a modern condo or a vintage Victorian? What color is it? Are there flowers? A big yard?

Get so specific with your information that you can see it in your mind.

Once you've got this all written down, look within your words for goals. What activities do you need to complete to make this dream life happen? You will have goals in different areas, such as:

- Self—where are you in each of the areas of self-care? What does your body look like?

- Finances—how much money are you earning? What does your bank account look like?

- Career/business—what work are you doing? What is the status of your business?

- Relationships—which relationships are you nurturing?

- Community—are you volunteering? How are you a part of your community?

Now you can begin to write goals based on the information you've extracted from a little bit of dreaming.

On the worksheet, you will be asked why you want the goal. This is important if you want to accomplish the goal. The why is what will drive you to accomplish the goal in the first place. Your why must be strong and it should drive you to keep working.

Next, you're asked to set a deadline. This helps you stay on target and helps you keep from putting off working toward your goal.

You'll also see a place to set action steps to accomplish your goal. These can be thought of as mini-goals and, while it isn't on the worksheet, I encourage you to set some rewards for yourself as you reach these milestones.

Next, you'll identify what motivates you to reach this goal. This goes with your why, but might be a little different. Think it through. Know what's pushing you. Are you sick of working in a job you hate? Are you tired of wishing for a thinner body?

The next important step is to identify potential roadblocks. There will be roadblocks to achieving your goals. There is no doubt about it, but if you think about those road- blocks now, you can plan a way around them.

Imagine taking a trip. You have a paper map, but it doesn't show road construction. If you get into Waze or another navigational app on your phone, however, it will warn you of possible travel problems ahead of time so you can plan a route around.

Knowing how to avoid a roadblock is a huge time-saver, as well as a great way to keep the roadblock from tripping you up as you make this journey!

Your next step is to identify a final reward. What will be the ultimate reward you give yourself for reaching this goal? Make it something that will motivate you!

Finally, think about what it will feel like to reach this goal. What emotions will you experience? Relief? Pride? Satisfaction? Think about how great it will feel to make this happen!

Goal Worksheet

What is your goal?

Why do you want to achieve this goal?

What is your deadline to complete this goal?

What action steps are required to meet this goal?
(Don't forget to set rewards!)

What motivates you toward this goal?

What might be a roadblock toward achieving this goal?

What reward can you give yourself for reaching this goal?

What will it feel like to achieve this goal?

Daily Routine

Daily Tasks

- _____
- _____
- _____
- _____
- _____
- _____
- _____
- _____
- _____
- _____
- _____
- _____

Habits to Add

- _____
- _____
- _____

Daily Self-Care Activities

- _____
- _____
- _____

Hour

7 _____

8 _____

9 _____

10 _____

11 _____

12 _____

1 _____

2 _____

3 _____

4 _____

5 _____

6 _____

7 _____

8 _____

9 _____

10 _____

How to Complete a Weekly Evaluation

The next worksheet in your workbook is a weekly evaluation. I encourage you to complete this every week. Every day, things happen to help us learn. The lesson might be as simple as moving a chair out of the way so you don't stub your toe on it, or it could be a big lesson, like how to be a better listener or when it's time to move on in a relationship.

Some lessons are fun to learn and others aren't, but learning isn't always intended to be a party. Unfortunately, instead of looking at the things in our life as learning opportunities, we use negative words like mistake and screw-up.

Part of the purpose of a weekly evaluation is to help you look back over the week for the learning opportunities, both from the good things that happened and the not-so-good things. The worksheet is broken down into the following questions.

 What are my accomplishments from last week? What did I learn?

Review the things you did last week that were good, or even great! What happened? Why was it so good? Who was around? How did it make you feel? The win doesn't need to be huge. It can be something as easy as getting an A on an exam or turning in a report that your boss loved.

What's important is to take the time to notice the wins in your life. Too often, we focus on the losses—the mistakes—the challenges. Instead of noticing that we did some things pretty well, we dwell on the problems and feel stuck in what felt like a hot mess.

 What was my biggest challenge last week? What did I learn?

This is not an opportunity to start beating yourself up. Instead, honestly look at areas in which you faced a challenge. This doesn't need to be something negative. Not all challenges are bad, in fact, no challenge is bad if you look at it as a learning opportunity.

Your challenge might have been learning how to balance a new work schedule or adjusting your routine because something changed. Your challenge could also be something you truly struggled with, and this is good! It means you have the opportunity to review everything with a new eye now that the situation has likely passed.

Remember to take the time to write about what you learned from the experience! That's the biggest win of all!

Score yourself in four pillar areas of yourlife

There are four pillar areas of your life to consider when making this evaluation:

Health & Well Being
How well did you eat last week? Were your meals mostly fast food or did you prepare healthy meals? Did you get some exercise? Did you drink plenty of water?

Business/Career & Income
This feels pretty broad, but think about your career and/or your business, especially if you're a business owner. How did the last week go? Were sales up or down? Is your career where you want it to be? If not, are you moving in the right direction to get it where you want it to be?

Relationships & Connections
This isn't just about a relationship with a guy, but all your relationships. Did you enjoy a great girls' night out with your friends? Do you feel as if you let a friend down or vice versa? Did you make some new connections?

Spirituality & Self
This is where you write about how well you took care of yourself and your soul in the past week. Regardless of what religion, if any, you practice, we all have some level of spirituality we practice. How well did you take care of your mind, body and soul over the past week?

What am I committed to in the upcoming week?

This can be anything. What will propel you toward a goal? Based on what you've learned about last week's accomplishments and challenges, what can you do to improve your scores in those four life areas? What is important to you, but wasn't on your radar last week?

Make sure to block out time on your calendar for whatever you commit to so the week doesn't pass by without any progress being made. Adding them to your calendar makes them real and helps you form a commitment to them.

 ## Where can I add fun, adventure and spontaneity into my week?

Everyone needs to take time out for some fun. It's part of your self-care routine. This is something else you should pencil into your calendar. Make time to enjoy time with a friend, go shopping, spend time on a hobby, or do whatever it is that makes you happy.

 ## What is my intention for the upcoming week?

Assign a theme to the upcoming week. It might be something like mindfulness or focus, then write it down so you remember it throughout the week!

Weekly Evaluation

What was my biggest accomplishment last week?
What did I learn from it?

What was my biggest challenge last week?
What did I learn from it?

How well did you do in each of these areas last week? Score yourself on a scale of zero to five, with zero indicating you did very poorly and 5 meaning you did great!

- Health & Well Being

- Business/Career & Income

- Relationships & Connections

- Spirituality & Self

What is the reason for the lowest score?

What is the reason for the highest score?

Where can I add fun, adventure and spontaneity into my week?

What is my intention for next week?

Overcoming Barriers

A couple of worksheets back, you worked on creating some goals. That's all well and good, but now, you must work on making a commitment to reach those goals. Unfortunately, there are often barriers or obstacles to achieving your goals.

For example, if you set a goal to lose ten pounds a week before Thanksgiving, there is an obvious barrier. This doesn't mean it's an impossible goal, it means you recognize the barrier and formulate a plan to overcome it.

Now, before you get aggravated with me, let me say that I would never tell you to avoid eating all those yummy foods on Thanksgiving! I'm saying that recognizing the potential hurdle before you need to jump over it allows you to plan ahead.

Instead of filling your plate twice, fill it once with small amounts of everything you want to eat.

The truly important thing about overcoming an obstacle is your attitude toward it. If you go into it with an attitude of "I can't do this," that's what will happen, but if you go into it with an attitude of "I can overcome this!", you will!

Sometimes, an obstacle might feel scary, or it might make you feel ashamed for some reason. Fear kicks your fight or flight instincts into high gear. Shame is an emotion that encourages you to hide and avoid.

Regardless of what negative emotion you feel, you must learn to recognize it and push through it. There are wonderful things on the other side!

Other obstacles might come from playing either the victim or the blame game. Neither is productive and neither will propel you toward what you want. Playing the victim means you're not accepting any responsibility for what goes on in your life. It plays so nicely with the blame game, "I can't lose weight because my parents gave me bad genes."

I'm not geneticist, but I don't believe there is a 'fat gene'. Chances are, your parents raised you with unhealthy habits, but this doesn't mean you're doomed. It means you're a grown-up now and it's time to take responsibility for what you do with your health.

Obstacles are an opportunity to grow—to solve a puzzle, they aren't threats or problems. So the true task is to change your language. Your other task is to understand one very important thing: if you're emotional, you cannot think logically. Those two cannot co-exist.

The next worksheet will provide you with some tools to overcome any barriers that might pop up when you're working toward a goal.

 # Overcoming Barriers Worksheet

Which goal are you working toward?

What emotion(s) are you experiencing about this goal?

Why do you think you feel that way? Is there history that causes you to feel this way? What are the barriers that first come to mind?

S.T.O.P.

This is an acronym for **S**top, **T**ake a step back, **O**bserve and **P**roceed. Observe your emotions. If your best friend was experiencing this right now, what would you say to her? How would you help her?

Accept

Every goal has obstacles, otherwise, you would probably already have achieved it. Instead of fighting obstacles and labeling them with negative words, accept obstacles as part of the process. Write a little note of acceptance to yourself.

Accept Your Emotions

Too many times, we try to shove our emotions down and not feel them, but this doesn't solve anything, as you probably already know. Take some time and self-soothe. Instead of letting your emotions tell you to put the brakes on, calm yourself and then proceed. You have control over your emotions. You always have had control, but now, you can learn how to practice that control and reel them in. Feel it and let it go. How can you self-soothe when your emotions flare as you try to reach this goal?

Be Flexible

Many times you see one—and only one—clear path to achieving your goal, but as those obstacles arise, it might be necessary to wander onto a new path. This is okay. How you reach your goal isn't as important as the achievement itself. If you need to take a few days off and restart, it's okay. Just adjust your timeline out a little further. The idea is not to allow obstacles to end the pursuit of your dreams! What are some possible alternate pathways to achieving your goal?

What is the Lesson?

Obstacles provide a learning opportunity. What is the learning opportunity associated with this obstacle?

Who can help?

Who can help you reach your goal? Do you need expert advice or someone to hold you accountable? Who is that person?

Smaller Goals

On your goals worksheet, you have a place for action steps. These are smaller goals that you can work toward. Make sure you complete that part of the worksheet so you can celebrate smaller wins!

Note On the next page is a physical self-care calendar. You will also find a copy of this calendar in your workbook, or you can draw your own.

Physical Self-Care Calendar

Month

Sunday	Monday	Tuesday	Wednesday	Thursday	Friday	Saturday

Physical Self-Care Ideas

You may already have some great ideas for physical self-care, but let me share a few that I dug up for you as well:

- Stretch your body
- Do breathing exercises
- Take a quick walk around the block (this is GREAT for stress & anxiety)
- Do Yoga
- Drink plenty of water
- Do a workout (also great for stress & anxiety)
- Get a massage
- Spend some time in nature
- Lie down on your stomach and scream all your frustrations out into your pillow
- Go dancing—even if it's in your living room
- Allow yourself to sleep in
- Get out of bed and prepare for the day
- Eat a balanced diet
- Wrap up in a blanket, even better, a weighted blanket (great for anxiety)

- Play in the rain
- Cook a meal you enjoy and then linger through it
- Take a walk on the beach
- Bake something tasty
- Take a hot shower or soak in a hot bath
- Smile and hold it for 20-30 seconds
- Go to the zoo
- Watch your favorite show or movie
- Plant something
- Put on clothing that makes you feel comfy and snug
- Create a zen space
- Squeeze a stress ball or knead something
- Clean a space in your home—de-clutter it
- Go for a swim, hike or bike ride
- Explore an unfamiliar area of your city
- Take a drive through the countryside and enjoy the view
- Take a nap
- Turn off the electronics
- Check in with your body—is there pain or tension? Try to release it
- Use a foot bath to relax and take care of your feet

Emotional
Self-Care

Emotional Self-Care

While physical self-care is about taking care of your body, emotional self-care focuses on your feelings, your conscious inner being and your intellect.

We all have emotional needs, but often, we set them aside in lieu of other's needs. Sometimes, we set them aside because feelings can be painful and can stir emotions that we don't know how to deal with healthily.

When you practice emotional self-care, you're taking care of your emotional needs by identifying your feelings and learning how to honor and accept them, moving forward in a healthy way, instead of through avoidance.

Signs that your emotional self-care is lacking include feeling frustrated or burned out. You might feel as if you've dug a deep hole and you can't seem to find the ladder to climb back out.

In this section of your self-care journey, you'll find worksheets and tips to help you:

• Protect yourself from the negative energy of others

• Create healthy boundaries

- Stop saying "Sorry" when it's not warranted

- Ask for help when you're feeling overwhelmed

- Stop over-explaining yourself

- Learn to experience and allow yourself to feel your emotions, instead of run from them

- Give yourself compassion and the grace to try again when things don't go as planned

- Know your emotions—the triggers and why you respond the way you do

- Develop a healthy support system

- Create an emotional toolbox

- Practice gratitude

- Accept compliments

This section is full of ways in which you can learn to take care of this aspect of your life.

Protecting Your Energy from Others

Too often, we come across people who spew negative energy. This person could be a friend, family member or perfect stranger. It doesn't matter because the negativity is toxic, regardless of where it comes from.

This toxic energy is damaging, especially if it's coming from someone close to you and you experience it frequently. It doesn't really matter whether the negative energy is specifically directed at you in the form of bullying and put-downs or it's just general negativity. It's toxic.

When someone is constantly bullying you or putting you down, the words begin to sink in, as does your reaction to them. They become stored in your subconscious as truths. "You're worthless" becomes something you're accustomed to hearing, and it might even become something you say to yourself.

Most of us have at least one person in our lives like this, often a family member. While I'm not encouraging you to cut family out of your life, what I do suggest is distancing yourself from someone like that.

Mary and her mother have had a toxic relationship for Mary's entire life. Jean, her mother, comes from a long line of negative energy women so this is quite natural for her. A few years ago, someone pointed out how toxic the relationship was, but Mary couldn't cut her mom out of her life.

Instead, Mary began to recognize her mother's toxic behaviors and learned how to manage her responses. When her mother became verbally or emotionally abusive, Mary recognized that this was her mother's problem to solve, not hers. She also started distancing herself when she saw the behavior emerging. Today, Mary and her mom have a solid relationship, but Mary is very quick to recognize when it's time to let the relationship cool for a few days until her mom can reset. By casually walking away or avoiding her mom when she begins to act out, she's sending a silent signal that the behavior is not okay.

If the negative energy comes from a friend or acquaintance, it's probably time to cut your losses and seek out more positive-energy friends.

The problem with negative energy is that it breeds. Think about the last time you and your girlfriends got together. Once someone started the 'dump on everyone' session, everyone chimed in and before you knew it, you had one big 'ole bitch session.

If you were alone, would you have initiated that negative thought train? It's important to begin sending your mind the signal that negativity won't be tolerated any longer.

On the following worksheet, you can work through some strategies to become more positive. You can also find this worksheet in the workbook.

Overcoming Negativity with Positive Thoughts

We don't see things as they are, we see things as we are.
—Anais Nin

Recall a recent situation when you felt like the whole thing just went wrong. Now, take a few moments to find one good thing about that situation. Next, still thinking about that situation, what is one thing you could have done differently to reach the desired outcome? What is one thing you can learn from this situation? If it was a friend going through this situation, what would you say to him or her to help them feel better about it?

Ask yourself whether you should take this negative thought seriously. Is what you're thinking true, or is it just a negative rut you've gotten stuck in? Are you tired? Hungry? These can help negative thoughts creep in. Are you focused on one tiny mistake, blowing it up way bigger than it should be?

What are the top three sources of negativity in your life? These could be people, places or things. It might be the news or a negative friend. It could be someone at work or someone you run into frequently, like a store clerk.

1.

2.

3.

What can you do to spend less time around these three sources in the upcoming week?

If you're blowing something out of proportion, ask yourself, "Will this matter in 5 years? Will it matter in 5 weeks?

Become mindful of this moment, right here and now. Shake yourself out of ruminating over past mistakes or anxiously worrying about the future. What's going on right now? You can do this by focusing on your breathing and taking a moment to observe your surroundings.

Be grateful. There are gratitude pages in the workbook, but find two things that you are grateful for in this moment.

1.

2.

Take time to be kind and compassionate to someone else. Bring positivity to others.

Why You Need Boundaries

Everyone needs boundaries. You can think of boundaries as the rules you're setting up to make sure people treat you as you deserve to be treated. Before you argue with me, you do deserve to be treated well and if you have no boundaries, you're probably not being treated well by everyone in your life.

Boundaries follow your values. For example, if you value being on time because you feel it's disrespectful to be late, you would have a boundary that helps you make sure you're on time.

But, your friend, Becky, is always late and she wants to drive both of you to the Yoga class you've just signed up for. You know, as sure as the sun will rise and set tomorrow, that Becky will be late for class. You have two choices, you can gracefully bow out of riding with her or you can accept her offer, but lay down a boundary. The first would look something like this:

"Becky, I'd love to ride together, but I have some things do to before class, so I'll just drive myself. Thank you though for offering!"

That is perfectly acceptable, kind and not accusing her of anything. Or, if you want to accept with a boundary, you can say this:

"Okay, Becky, let's ride together, but if it seems you're running

*behind, I'll go ahead and leave fifteen minutes before class starts.
That way, you won't be late by swinging by my place."*

This is a graceful way to establish a boundary. You've told her that if she isn't there fifteen minutes before class starts, you're driving yourself. You didn't accuse or get nasty with her, you just stated how you'd handle the situation.

Now, if Becky is a good boundary buster, as some are, she might come back with something like this:

"Oh no, Becky, don't drive yourself! I'll be there for sure! And even if I'm not there by quarter-to, we won't be very late. It'll be fine. I'll see you later!"

This is where you must strengthen your resolve! Be firm in your boundary. If she doesn't show by the designated time, you drive yourself. If she stops by to pick you up and you're not there, she just learned that you're a woman of your word.

You didn't do anything wrong! This doesn't mean she won't try to make you feel guilty for standing your ground, in fact, she probably will. Do not cave. You held to your boundary and that's what's important. It's okay to make the same arrangement with her next week, but you must stick to your guns. Leave at the designated time. Don't *give her one more minute*, because that one more minute turns into ten or fifteen minutes and you're both late.

It may take a few weeks for her to recognize that you mean

what you say, but that's on her, not you. Your job is to teach her how to treat you. Showing up late is disrespectful. It tells the other person that they aren't important enough to be on time for. In this instance, she is being disrespectful to you, the Yoga instructor and everyone in the class.

The worksheet on the following page (or in your workbook) will help you begin to think through boundaries. You will need to go through it a few times in order to get the boundaries you need to have. Try not to set more than a couple at a time.

At first, these will feel uncomfortable to you, especially if your friends and family are accustomed to using you as a doormat, but you're no doormat!

The more you practice holding onto your boundaries, the easier it will become. People who are true friends will learn to treat you within your boundaries. People who were only friends with you to use you will get mad and exit your life.

Say good riddance to them—they weren't really friends anyway.

I want to help you understand one more thing before you dip into the worksheet, and that's consequences.

There are natural consequences and consequences you establish. Your teenager not getting up in time to catch the bus, thus forcing him to walk to school is a natural consequence. Your friend Becky showing up late missing you because you drove yourself is a you-based consequence.

Natural consequences are cool because you're off the hook. There is just a consequence and you don't have a thing to do with it. It's like kids and homework—they don't do the homework, they don't get good grades. They don't get good grades, they can't get into the college or program they want to get into. It's a hard lesson to learn and it takes a while to undo it, but you have to let them learn it on their own.

 ## How to Set Healthy Boundaries

In order to set healthy boundaries, it's important first to determine where you need them. To do that, answer these questions.

I feel angry when...

I feel frustrated when...

I feel hurt when...

I feel I've been taken advantage of when...

I feel disrespected when...

Which of those above situations is most bothersome at this time? That's the one to focus on for the rest of this worksheet.

In order to feel better when this situation arises or when I am with this person, I need to set a boundary which...

What will you say to someone when you declare this boundary to them? Frame these statements from your point of view, like this: "I feel frustrated when..." or, "I feel disappointed when..." It's difficult for someone to argue with your feelings, and you're not accusing them of anything.

What are the consequences when someone breaks a boundary you have set and declared to them? Will there be natural consequences, such as, "If you don't get out of bed on time, you will be late for work", or will there be consequence you initiate like, "If you're late to pick me up the next time, I'll just drive myself." Know what your 'or else' is for the boundary.

No More Saying "I'm Sorry"
(Unless you really should!)

If you owe someone an apology, you should, by all means, say you're sorry, but for many, saying, "I'm sorry" becomes a default response. This is not a good thing.

When you apologize too much, especially for things you don't need to apologize for, people think less of you. It is a sign of low confidence and a need to garner acceptance.

While you might think apologizing all the time makes you seem nice and caring, what it actually does is give silent permission to specific types of people to treat you badly or even abuse you.

Additionally, when you apologize for everything, it lessens the impact of an apology when it is truly warranted. For example, you don't need to apologize for things like:

- Sneezing
- Standing in someone's way when you can't really stand anywhere else
- Someone bumping into you
- Being interrupted

Sometimes, 'excuse me' works instead of 'I'm sorry' in those instances, but again, sometimes what happened isn't your fault and you don't need to say anything.

Listening to someone apologize all the time is also kind of annoying. Have you ever been around the person who uses an apology before canceling plans or breaking up with you? In that instance, "I'm sorry" adds to the hurt. If they're so sorry, why are they doing it? It deepens the feeling of rejection, instead of lessening it.

In a study published by the European Journal of Social Psychology, they found that people who didn't apologize for every little thing were more confident, had a greater feeling of power and integrity.

The bottom line is that like anything else, you should use "I'm sorry" rather sparingly. If you bump into someone, it's perfectly polite to apologize but if they bump into you, don't.

Your apology should be reserved for the instances in which you truly mean it and it's really up to you to say something. If the situation is beyond your control, like a sneeze, saying I'm sorry has little impact.

Part of your journey to take better care of yourself includes growing your confidence. The next worksheet will help you overcome the need to apologize all the time. You can also find this worksheet in the workbook.

How to Stop Apologizing

Is this you? Before you get too worried about apologizing all the time, examine your behaviors and tendencies. Do you apologize too much? Try keeping a count of the number of times you apologize throughout the day.

When should you really apologize? You owe an apology if you deliberately do something to hurt or offend someone. In that instance, be brave and strong enough to issue the required apology. This will serve to strengthen your relationship, where as letting a hurt go by without an apology will weaken it. It sucks to admit you're wrong, but people will think more of you for it.

Learn to alter your language away from 'I'm sorry'. If your boss catches a mistake you made in a report, instead of saying 'I'm sorry', say something like, "Thank you for catching that, I'll be sure to fix it right away." If you're in someone's way, instead of saying, 'I'm sorry', try, "Here, allow me to move out of your way." Many times, there are other phrases you can insert that better fit the situation. Try to think of a couple that would work in recent situations where you said 'I'm sorry'.

Learn how to say 'No'. Sometimes, 'I'm sorry' can be used instead of a solid 'No'. If someone at work asks you to help them finish their project but you've got your own work to do, simply say, "I really can't help you this time, but ask me again, okay?" If your friends want you to go to lunch with them but you have other plans or don't want to, you can say, "Maybe next time. I can't make it this time." We feel the need to apologize and

explain ourselves away when it's not necessary. Practice a few
ways in which you can bow out, instead of using 'I'm sorry'.

Below are a few ways in which we use "I'm sorry", when it's not
necessary. Try to eliminate these from you repertoire.

- "I'm sorry! Was I in your way?"—Just say 'Excuse me'
  instead

- "I'm sorry. This is a stupid question but..."—No need to
  apologize for asking a question

- I'm sorry. I just feel as if..." Never apologize for your
  feelings

- "I'm sorry—I look like a mess today" You owe nobody an
  apology for how you look

- "I'm sorry. I need to stay home tonight and relax" You
  don't need to apologize for self-care

- "I'm sorry, can you help me?" Don't apologize for not
  understanding

- "I'm sorry—Tom had a bad day. He didn't mean it" You owe
  no apology for someone else's bad behavior

- "I'm sorry I didn't call you back right away" Don't
  apologize for being busy doing something else; try "I was a
  bit busy when you called, but now I'm available to talk."

- "I'm sorry" when someone shares a bad experience—in
  this instance, take the blame off of yourself by adding a few
  words, "I'm sorry that happened"

How and When to Ask for Help

You might feel as if asking for help makes you look weak or helpless but it doesn't. That old, 'I am woman hear me roar' mentality that is being ingrained in so many women today can make you feel as if asking for help lessens your ability to roar.

But what if you're getting in your own way by not asking for help? When you perceive asking for help to be a negative thing, you will hurt your chances to do great things and become a stronger person.

Asking for help does not mean you're stupid or inadequate. It means you recognize your limitations and you need help with something specific. You are not a burden when you ask for help. That person you're asking may need you to return the favor, and you know you would in a heartbeat!

 ## When to ask for help

Confident people recognize that asking for help is not a sign of weakness or inadequacy. They understand that trying to do everything by themselves isn't the best use of their time, energy or skills.

A general contractor hires electricians, plumbers and HVAC

people because he knows they can do those jobs faster and better.

A doctor hires nurses and assistants to do blood pressures and vital checks so he can use his expertise to help his patients with things nurses and assistants can't.

It's okay to ask someone for help when you know they can be an asset to your project. If you know their skill-set enhances your work, it's perfectly reasonable to ask.

I'm always going up to Maine to help my sister with her new house. Why? Because I'm a contractor and I know how to do that stuff. My brother-in-law helps, but he knows his limitations and leaves the stuff in my expertise for me. I recently spent several weekends up there redoing a bathroom my sister set aside for my mom and stepdad so that it was more friendly to older users. It's what I do.

 ## How to ask for help

Show that you've tried
In some instances, you may have tried to do something yourself first. You can say something like, "I tried unscrewing this thing-a-ma-jig over there to get the lid off, but it still seems stuck." This not only tells them you've tried, but it gives them some cues on how to help you. Help might be as easy as them saying, "Yes you need to unscrew that, but there's also one underneath that you need to address."

Let them know you've tried their advice before

If you always ask someone for help but rarely follow their advice, they'll be much less likely to insert themselves again. People are happy to help if they know you're likely to heed their advice.

Be sure to show your appreciation for their assistance!

Time your request appropriately

Being mindful of the other person's needs and schedule makes it easier for them to give you the 'yes' you need. If you know someone is at work, you can either wait until they're off, or you can form your request to acknowledge the time, "I know you're at work right now, but when you get home, I'd like to ask for your help with something."

Also, be mindful of their needs, "I know you're buried in your project right now. How about if I help you by taking X, Y and Z off your hands and then you can help me with my project. I'm really stuck on W and I know you're really good at that."

When someone recognizes that you're considering their needs, they'll be more likely to want to help.

Don't make them guess at what you want

When you ask someone for their assistance, make sure you explain exactly what it is you need help with. For example, if you're traveling with three small children and need help with a door, chances are most strangers would lend a hand if you ask, "Could you please hold that door open for me for a moment?"

Many people are just shy about offering help or they don't truly observe that you're struggling. They're happy to help once they recognize the need. This is a win-win because helping someone like that usually boosts the mood of the person helping.

Be quick to offer help yourself
Being a helper makes you more likely to ask for help. In addition, people are more likely to honor your request because they know you to be a helper-type.

 ## Don't be shy!

Knowing when and how to ask for help provides you with the ability to grow and learn. You gain the expertise of someone more knowledgeable and you're more likely to try it alone next time. That's a confidence booster!

How to Stop Over-Explaining

There are people who provide a curt yes or no as a response to anything, and if that won't work, you might eek three or four words out of them, then there are those who feel the need to explain things in such depth that the other person's mind has long- ago drifted off. There's a healthy middle ground that I hope to help you find today.

Why people over-explain

Over-explaining is a sign of either low self-esteem or people pleasing behavior. Often, it's the result of experiencing a child-hood when one or both parents were unable to meet and/or understand the emotional needs of the child.

Sometimes, parents are too wrapped up in their own anxiety, depression or general dysfunction to even notice the distress of a child. They can't help it. Still, if parents don't show empa-thy, are self-centered, or lack the ability to really listen to their children, the children will feel frustrated and misunderstood.

Enter over-explaining.

Most of the time, when someone is an over-explainer, they're anxious about feeling misunderstood. So much of their past was just that way and now, they don't want to repeat the pattern. Instead, they adopt another pattern—over-explaining.

Why it's important to stop

Sometimes, when you over-explain something to someone, it makes them feel stupid. They got you on the first three words, but you ramble on, as if they didn't have a clue what you just said. Nobody wants to make another person feel stupid.

Over-explaining can signal that you're over-thinking something. This can come from too much worry or rumination, also behaviors that don't serve you well.

When you over-explain, it can make you look as if you're stressed out because you can't get your point across. This, in turn, makes the listener feel stressed.

Some might perceive you as being confused, which, if it goes on long enough, will confuse them as well.

It's important to recognize that past patterns of behavior from others in your life are not predictors of future behaviors of new people, and yet, by over-explaining, you're treating them as if they're the ones who didn't get you as a child.

How to stop over-explaining

First, recognize that the quantity of words you use to convey your message isn't as important as the clarity of the words you use.

Joe: *Are you a cat person or a dog person? Me? I'm a dog person.*

Molly: *Oh, I don't much care for animals. They have dander which I'm allergic to, and then there's the hair all over the place, and let's not even get into litter boxes or trotting around the neighborhood with pooh bags.*

Joe has moved on to thinking about which team to root for in this week's Sunday Night Football game. All Molly needed to say was, "I'm not really a big animal person."

As you prepare your thoughts, ask yourself this one big question: are the words you're about to use truly important to the conversation? Can you sum up your thoughts in fewer, more concise words?

If you have the chance, practice what you'll say to someone before you say it. Sometimes this is possible, sometimes it isn't. Practice using precise words to convey your message.

Be mindful of your words and whether you're over-thinking the situation. Sometimes, there is a concern over being accepted by the person you're speaking to. Instead, consider this—if they don't like what you said, it's on them, not you.

You cannot control how someone reacts to what you say or do, and yet, we try to do this with the words we use. In fact, many anxious moments come about because we're over-thinking an upcoming conversation.

Emily wanted to talk to Mike about moving in together, but she was worried that he might not think they were ready. He seemed like he was ready. They stayed together at one apartment or the other almost every night already. It seemed silly to pay for two. But, what if he got angry and decided to break up with her? What if he thought she wasn't really the right girl for him and he'd just been stringing her along until a better option came along? She replayed the conversation between them over and over in her head, never with a positive ending. She over-thought it so much that she tabled the conversation because she decided he would dump her. Two weeks later, Mike suggested it and none of what she had worried about came to be.

Finally, practice being a better listener. If you're actively listening, you begin to understand that they do get what you're saying and your need to over-explain dissipates. Show the people in your life that you value their time and energy by paring down your words and saving the big drawn-out explanations for when they're truly needed.

How to Feel Your Emotions & Let Them Go

Many times, it seems easier to push emotions deep inside so we don't feel the pain they cause. If we ignore those feelings, they'll just go away, right?

Wrong. Ignoring your feelings doesn't make them go away at all, in fact, it may even deepen your pain. Not wanting to feel pain is very natural. Nobody wants to hurt, whether it's a sore joint from overuse or emotional pain. Pain is pain.

You may have been taught that your feelings weren't valid. This can happen when people ignore you when you express yourself.

Everything you feel is valid. Don't ever stop believing that! It isn't the feelings themselves that are the problem, it's how we receive them. Often, we receive feelings and we judge them or simply refuse to feel them. Do any of these sound familiar?

- I shouldn't feel this way

- Why can't I just stop?

- Suck it up! Don't be so weak!

- The person I want to be doesn't feel like this

- Geeze girl! Get your sh*% together already!

- I'm so stupid

- I don't have the right to feel this way

The problem with judging your emotions or avoiding them is that you miss out on the lesson to be learned. Emotions don't appear because you're weak. They're a signal that something is wrong. You're hurting in some way, perhaps a very valid reason, and you need to address where the pain is coming from. The emotions are merely the messenger of the problem.

Nobody can tell you that how you're dealing with something is right or wrong. Your way is your way.

Steve and Kevin are brothers who lost their sister, Sue, when she was just nineteen years old. She died of cystic fibrosis and had led a life filled with both pain and joy. Steve was older than Sue while Kevin was younger, but all three were close to one another in age and close as siblings.

When Sue passed, Kevin was distraught. He truly felt and experienced his emotions. He went to visit his girlfriend and cried in her arms for several minutes. Steve, on the other hand, barely shed a tear. After her funeral and burial, Kevin would visit her grave, but Steve never did.

Everyone always said that Steve's way of dealing with his sister's death was wrong, but who were they to tell him how to feel? To this day, he has had no negative impact on how he handled her passing, which was nearly forty years ago now. He dealt with it his way and his family doesn't know how he grieved in private.

Your feelings are your own. Someone else cannot and should not tell you how to feel them, when to feel them or how deeply to feel them.

It's important for you to understand that your pain is the messenger. Emotional pain is just like physical pain. It's a warning signal that something is out of whack somewhere. It's nature telling you that something needs to be addressed.

The pain isn't wrong. It's the messenger and you've certainly heard that you should never shoot the messenger! Doing so only begins to disable the messenger and that is never a good thing!

On the next couple of pages, you'll find a worksheet designed to help you work through your emotions, instead of stuffing them deeper. When you're experiencing emotional pain and your inclination is to avoid it, turn to these worksheets instead. Of course, this worksheet is also available in your workbook!

Dealing with Emotional Pain

When you feel emotional, check in with these questions:

1. What happened? What was the trigger for this emotion?

2. What is the truth, versus the thoughts and beliefs that are swarming through my head right now? In what negative way have these false thoughts and beliefs harmed me in the past?

3. What is the story I'm telling myself about what it means to feel this way? Sometimes, you may attach your self-worth to things like how you're dressed, where you work or live and what you drive. These emotions might be playing with that narrative in a negative way, and yet, self-worth is not tied to your job, clothing, home or car.

This story might work out something like one of these examples:

I feel hurt comes across as feeling like a cry baby or being over-sensitive.

I feel angry might be perceived as lacking self-control or feeling difficult or even crazy.

I am disappointed might come off as being pessimistic.

I am afraid often feels like admitting you're weak.

None of these are true, but they're the stories we tell ourselves.

4. Accept your feelings. Once you do this—once you allow yourself to both feel and accept those emotions, you are well on your way to letting them go. Avoiding emotions doesn't make them go away. It simply makes them fester and negatively impact your life. Feeling them and allowing them to flow through you gives you the power to let them go. Only through feeling your emotions can you be free of them.

5. Re-frame your experience. Instead of judging or shaming yourself for feeling the way you do, re-frame it in a way that

helps you move forward in a healthy way.

Can you love yourself enough, right now, to allow yourself to have this experience? Emotions are opportunities to move forward, they aren't examples of sliding backward.

Emotions will come, regardless of who you are and what you've experienced in your past. You're only human and you deserve to be able to feel this.

6. FEEL it. It might help to say this to yourself as you're experiencing the emotion: *It's okay for me to feel this.* Repeat it, over and over, until the emotion passes. You must allow it to flow through you so it doesn't get stuck in you!

7. Look for the lesson in feeling the emotion. What can you take away from the experience?

Developing Self-Compassion & Kindness

We say things to ourselves that we would never dream of saying to another individual, whether stranger, friend or family member. Developing self-compassion can be a difficult thing, especially if someone was raised in an abusive or unloving home.

Self-compassion is defined as a way of relating to yourself with kindness, but is not the same thing as arrogance or conceit. Treating yourself with kindness is an act of love. Conceit and arrogance indicate a *lack* of self-love.

When you are self-compassionate, you are kind and gentle toward yourself. You are supportive and understanding. You might be thinking, "Hey, this is easy. I'm supportive of myself." But are you? Or are you more judgmental? We've already spent a moment or two on how to eradicate judgmental thoughts.

We all have them. I'm sure you have judged yourself in the past. With self-compassion, you don't judge yourself, but instead provide unconditional acceptance of who you are and what you do. This doesn't mean that you suddenly decide that hurting someone is okay. It means that you recognize the difference between making a bad decision and being a bad person in general.

Everyone makes poor decisions from time to time. That's how we learn. The difference between those who practice self-compassion and those who don't is whether you believe that every poor decision makes you an even worse person than the last.

Studies over the last ten years or so have begun to show a relationship between practicing self-compassion and having healthy psychological well-being. In other words, when you cut yourself some slack, your mental health is better for it.

People who practice self-compassion are shown to have greater self-esteem, social connectedness, emotional intelligence, happiness and overall satisfaction with their life. These same individuals have lower anxiety, stress, depression, shame and fear of failure. Doesn't that sound nice?

People with little or no self-compassion don't fare well in relationships. If you don't love yourself, others won't treat you kindly either. You set the standard for what you will accept as treatment of yourself. Others see this lack of kindness and treat you in the same way. Additionally, we draw to ourselves those who are most like us. So if you lack self-compassion, those around you will too.

With self-compassion, you're less likely to depend on others to help you define your sense of self-worth.

Let's imagine for a moment that you won the lottery. You have unlimited resources to do whatever you want for the foreseeable future. You decide to take a journey—to travel the world and you want to take someone along with you.

Who would you choose? Someone who is constantly berating you for each poor decision you make or someone who is kind and supportive?

Easy, right? You'd choose the kind and supportive one. Well, you are on a journey. Life is a journey. We never truly know what will happen when we get out of bed every day. We may have a plan, but plans don't always work out for one reason or another.

In this journey of life that we're all on, we have one constant companion—our mind. It's always there, talking, prodding, encouraging, back-talking, berating. Is your mind supportive of you? When you listen to what you're saying to yourself, are those words you would say to anyone else?

You have a filter through which you view life. It's based on your life experiences up to that moment. Remember this quote:

We don't see things as they are, we see things as we are.
-Anais Nin

As you consider the questions and statements on the next worksheet, keep this quote in mind. To some extent, your values play a role in this whole process. Those who raised you instilled their values on you, but as an adult, you have the opportunity to develop your own values—your own moral compass and perspectives or filters through which you view life. Following the worksheet on self-compassion, you'll find one on cultivating your own set of values, unique to you.

These values will help you begin to establish a set of rules by which you will live your life. Your challenge is to take those values and begin to anchor your behaviors to them, but not to become so well anchored that you beat yourself up every time you temporarily lose sight of your values.

Values are a great compass, as long as you don't use them to further your self-abuse. Self-compassion, again, means recognizing that a slip-up is a poor decision, but it doesn't make you a bad person.

Learning to forgive yourself for mistakes, acknowledging the need to try again and do better, cutting yourself some well-deserved slack, will help you feel much better about your life and will enable you to begin to form lasting, healthy relationships with yourself and those around you.

 Developing Self-Compassion

1. Forgiveness

In order to practice self-compassion, an important first step is to learn to forgive yourself. You are human and, therefore, not perfect. Nobody is perfect, yet many of us hold ourselves to a very high standard of perfection and any time we don't meet that standard, we beat ourselves up. People around you who love you do so because you're human, because of how you treat them, not because they see you as perfect. They just see you as perfect for them.

Put a few notes in key places, like on your desk at work, your mirror at home or other places you see often. These notes should remind you to be kind and compassionate to yourself and maybe even to forgive yourself until you get better at it. You can also write a letter to yourself, forgiving yourself for either a lifetime of mistakes that need to be forgiven, or for something specific that's eating at you. You can do this whenever you feel you need to extend forgiveness.

2. Develop a mindset of growth and opportunity

Language is everything. You might read that more than once in this journey. When you find yourself in a situation where you've made a poor choice, you are at a fork in the road. You can view this in a negative way or you can view it in a positive way. Negativity sees no opportunity for growth while positivity sees each new challenge as an opportunity to learn something new—to grow. Think about an obstacle you've faced recently. What is the opportunity for growth?

3. Express gratitude

Have you noticed that some of these are repeating themes? You don't need to write gratitude here, but remember to maintain a practice of daily gratitude statements. Try not to repeat the same gratitudes from one day to the next. Appreciate what you do have, instead of lamenting over what you don't have.

4. Be generous, but in the right way

Generosity can be overdone. Think about the last time you extended generosity to someone. Did it meet this criteria?

- You took your own needs into consideration before extending generosity

- You consciously chose the recipient of your generosity

- You considered the resources you have available before offering more than you may have to give

- You had the time and energy to extend that generosity

In the future, be sure to consider these before offering your generosity. When you give too much, you fail to take care of yourself as well, and that's what this whole journal is about!

5. Practice mindfulness

This is another recurring theme. When you are mindful of the here and now, you're less likely to be judgmental of the past or to place labels on yourself that don't apply. Take some time now to just sit for a few moments and enjoy each moment. What are the smells, the sights and the sounds of where you are? Just enjoy whatever is around you.

6. Treat yourself as you would a friend.

Think about the last time you were angry with yourself over something. If a friend had made this error in judgment, would you have treated them in the same way? Begin to recognize that you are a friend of yours and start treating yourself as such. What can you say to yourself now about that past situation? What would you say to that friend?

What are Your Values?

Use the following questions and statements to develop your own core values.

1. You might think you know what your values are, but suspend reality for a moment and act like you don't. Take a few moments to calm your mind and quiet the space you're in. If you need to relocate to do this activity, so be it.

2. You develop your own values—you cultivate them. You don't pick them off a list like apples off a tree, so instead of using a list, consider the following:

    Write about a meaningful moment in your life—a peak experience that stands out. What was happening to you? What was going on? What values were you honoring at that time?

    Think of a time when you felt angry, frustrated, disappointed or upset. What was going on? What were you feeling? Now, what is the opposite? What value was not being adhered to in that situation?

What is your personal code of conduct? What do you require in your life to feel fulfilled? Creativity? Financial security? Good health? Always learning? These are things that go beyond basic needs.

3.   Write the values you uncovered in those three exercises.

Next, group them into related themes. For example, you might have written exercise, healthy eating and taking care of yourself in those answers—they can be combined into self-care. What are the themes or core values you've come up with?

If you still have a rather large list, it's time to whittle it down. To do so, answer these questions:

What values are essential to your life today? Which values represent your primary way of being? What values support your inner self?

Your goal should be a solid list of five to ten values. Once you have them, create value statements for each. Use creative language like: *Health: I will live a life full of healthy eating and workout habits.*

Understanding Emotional Triggers & Your Response

Your beliefs about any given situation will determine how you react to it. Emotional triggers are experiences that draw us back into the past and dredge up old feelings. They can relate to personal relationships, work or life in general. You might not even realize they exist until someone touches a hot button.

Suzanna was divorced from an emotionally abusive man. She didn't realize that he had left her with emotional triggers until she began dating again. Out of the blue, a man would say or do something and she would find herself immediately irate. Suzanna knew her ex had emotionally abused her. After her divorce, she had set her mind to never allow that to happen again, so when another man innocently used a specific phrase her ex had used, it was like hitting a hot button inside her. For Suzanna, this was kind of an 'oh my' moment as she recognized what was happening. Of course, it took a couple of hot button hits before she recognized that she needed to deal with these triggers. In order to move on into a healthy relationship, she needed to identify those triggers and learn to control her responses.

Identifying the cause of your trigger is key in learning to let it go, which is what Suzanna had to do. She had to let go of the hurts of the past and also to forgive herself for allowing some-one to hurt her in that way.

Your triggers might not always be people. Triggers can be sit-uational as well.

Kurt and his brother, Marc both have social anxiety. Growing up, they would challenge one another to be the first to say "Hi" to a stranger when they were out as a way of trying to overcome their anxiety. Later, Kurt began dating Daisy. While Kurt is a quiet type of guy in general, Daisy is more outgoing, so he found himself in social situations that truly stirred his anxiety, but he was too embarrassed to say so. One evening, he attended a sporting event with Daisy and her family. After being at the game and then in the car for the ride home, Kurt's anxiety hit an all-time high. At a stop light just a couple of miles from his home, he got out of the car and started running. Startled, Daisy's mom called out, but Daisy knew of his anxiety and told her mom to let him go. Kurt's trigger was first the game and then, the ride home with Daisy's family. It was just too much socialization. Today, Kurt works in a very busy hospital and has overcome much of his social anxiety, but he did so by recognizing his triggers and learning how to manage them.

Other triggers are more internal. For many people, there is an anxiety over what other people think. This influences how they dress, where they live, what car they drive and sometimes even what profession they choose. Their life is so wrapped up in the opinions of others that they don't live a life true to themselves. This can cause emotional triggers to pop up without warning. This is telling you that you're more tuned in to the emotions of others than your own. You've set aside feeling your own stuff in lieu of feeling what you think others perceive about you. If you think you're disappointing a parent because you chose the wrong profession, you may feel disappointed instead of being proud you stood up for yourself. If you forgot to bring snacks to soccer practice, you might think other parents or coaches are judging you as incompetent. You feel incompetent, instead of recognizing that your boss made you work late and you weren't able to get the snack there in time.

You need to understand that everyone has emotional triggers. The difference between one person and the next is how you manage those triggers.

There is a worksheet coming up on learning to recognize emotional triggers, but along with that worksheet, continue writing in your journal. This worksheet is also in your workbook. If you're being honest with yourself, those triggers will show up on what you write. Read back through your previous entries with the eye of a stranger and see if you can unearth some of them. As you continue to write, look back every week or so to see what types of triggers may have appeared.

In order to move forward in dealing with your triggers, remember not to try to avoid the things that trigger you. Instead develop coping mechanisms or overcome the emotional pain associated with the trigger.

If you've led a life of feeling as if you've disappointed your parents over and over, it's time to recognize that you're an adult and you only need to live up to your own expectations. If they're disappointed, that's on them. You cannot control how others react.

When you recognize that something in your life is broken, you owe it to yourself to fix it. Self-care not only means being physically healthy, but taking care of your emotional health as well. Much of what is broken in us lies in our emotional health.

Taking care of you means giving yourself the opportunity to fix those broken areas and growing into the person you wish to be.

Be careful not to fall into the trap of believing that change is too difficult or too painful. You've already come across topics that address working through the painful stuff. You already know you'll be better for pushing through.

Again, if you feel at any time that you're suicidal or that you just can't move forward, I strongly urge you to seek professional help. I am a coach, not a therapist. A therapist will be much better equipped to help you with those challenges.

 Removing Emotional Triggers

In order to recognize and remove the barriers caused by emotional triggers, try these steps.

1. Understand that you, and only you, are responsible for your reactions. This is a toughie and I've angered more than one person by saying this, but if you don't believe this one

truth, you don't need to move forward. For every situation, you are reacting in a chosen way. It's time to shed the victim mentality and own your reactions.

Think back to a recent situation where you allowed your emotions to run amok. Perhaps someone pulled out in front of you in traffic and you yelled and flipped them the bird. What could you have done differently? If you had taken just a moment's breath and considered your reaction, what would you have done? Maybe the same thing, but maybe not. Either way, you at least controlled it.

2. Learn to recognize emotional reactions as they occur. Begin to recognize the signals. For example, when you feel anxious, your heart rate will increase, you may begin to feel sweaty, you might feel the need to flee the situation. If you're scared, you might hold your breath. Recognizing when your body begins to react is key in learning how to control that reaction. This isn't the time to judge those feelings, but to recognize them.

3. If the emotion is fear, anger or sadness, your next step is to look for the trigger. What just happened? Where are you? Who is around? What's going on? Think back to the last time you felt one of those and answer those questions about that situation.

4. As you begin to detect your triggers, you can learn to detect whether there is a real threat or not. In the case of Suzanna, the threat of her ex was gone and a new man was unintentionally saying or doing something that triggered the

emotion. She could manage this by recognizing that trigger and determining that there was no real threat any longer.

Looking back through some recent incidents, and in the next few weeks, begin to draft a list of things that trigger your emotions. These might include acceptance, respect, feeling valued, the need to be right, the need to be in control, order, wanting to feel included, and so on.

5. What are your top three triggers? Chances are, they're needs that you have, like acceptance. Begin to retrain yourself to recognize that being accepted by everyone isn't necessary for you to prosper in life. There will never come a time when everyone will accept you. Begin to lessen the importance of 100% acceptance. This will help your mind recognize that a lack of acceptance is not a threat to your well-being. If someone doesn't accept you, it's their loss.

6. Now that you've identified some triggers, it's time to choose how you want to react to them instead of just allowing a reaction to occur. If someone doesn't accept you, what do you want your reaction to be? Preparing for the situation before it occurs again helps you to react in a healthier and more beneficial way.

How to Develop a
Healthy Support System

A support system is there for you when you experience the normal ups and downs of life. You need someone to listen and provide honest feedback, versus whatever your mind might be telling you at the moment.

Having a support system can boost your well-being, provide you with better coping skills and help you live a longer, more productive life. Those are some pretty big bonuses! And, as if those aren't enough, people with a good emotional support system report less anxiety and depression.

The size of your support system isn't as important as the strength of the bond. You may find that support in close friends or family members. What's important is that this group helps you decrease stress, not increase it.

Isolation from others causes depression in adults. It sometimes comes from busying ourselves with relationships or work, especially if you make a conscious choice to become a stay-at-home mom or you work from home. Neither of these are poor choices, but they are circumstances that should encourage you to maintain connections instead of allowing them to wither and die.

It's important to recognize what a support system is and is not.

A support system is made up of people who provide support, respect and care. These people are honest with you in a way that is helpful, not harmful. They don't judge or ridicule you, but are there, in your corner, fighting for you. Their feedback is genuine and honest. They're not there to tell you what you want to hear, but what you need to hear. Their impact on your life is positive, all the time.

While many in your support system are close friends and family members, they can also be people in the community that you run into frequently, like clergy, pharmacists, physicians, baristas or even clerks in a store who've come to know you over time.

These people develop the ability to recognize when you're not quite yourself and may ask if everything is okay. They're not nosy—they're part of your support system. They care.

Your support system does not include people who tear you down or tear others down. This type of person falls into that negative category we talked about earlier. This isn't being supportive. It's damaging.

In the following worksheet, you will learn how to identify and grow your support system. This worksheet is also available in your workbook.

Developing & Growing Your Emotional Support System

1.   Who is already in your corner? Who stands up for you? Who is a positive influence? Include family, friends, neighbors, and acquaintances. Also include people in the community who know you. These people should:

     •   Make you feel respected

     •   Be someone you trust

     •   Bring out the best in you

     •   Help you feel good about yourself

     •   Positively interact with you and others

2.   Now, it's time to grow that support system. Where can you look for more people like this?

3.   What roadblocks have you put in place to discourage people from joining your support system? These might include low self-esteem and confidence, depression, misguided priorities, disorganization in life, or difficulty asking for help.

4.   Commit to using your support system. It's one thing to identify people who can be there for you, but it's another thing to actually commit to using them. If you've had trouble in the past asking for help, then doing so now can also be a challenge. Review your roadblocks and ask yourself how you can remove them. In what situations would a support system have been helpful? How did that roadblock prevent you from seeking that support?

Identify one situation you're facing right now where a support system would be beneficial. Who on your list can you turn to for that support? Prepare yourself to ask for that support by working through the roadblock that's currently stopping you.

5. As you begin healthily working with your support system, be mindful of anyone who is on your list but shouldn't be. This person likely takes more than they give. You want to be sure you're not that type of person as well. Having a support system means reciprocating that support. When those on your list need your support, be prepared to step in. Beware of any roadblocks you might already have that prevent you from doing so.

 How to Develop an Emotional Toolbox

I found it distressing to discover in researching this topic that many articles focus on helping children develop an emotional toolbox. Very few experts give time to helping adults develop one. Of course, this motivated me further!

Life hits hard some days, and despite many tools you've developed so far in this journal, you still need to prepare an emotional toolbox for yourself. Why?

Because you never know when life is going to hit. You may lose your job due to the economy or struggle with a personal relationship. Perhaps the COVID quarantine left you feeling isolated and depressed. Regardless of the cause, being able to turn to an already prepared emotional toolbox will help you cope.

As you're discovering, learning to manage your emotions is key in taking care of your emotional self-care. In doing this, you're developing resilience, or the ability to create more good than would be expected of you after experiencing something difficult. For example, you may have experienced abuse as a child, but rather than growing up to isolate and blame yourself for the experience, you dedicate yourself to helping children of abuse and get an advanced degree in psychology or social work.

Right now, you might feel as if you're shattered—dispersed in a million pieces that you can't seem to put together. It may feel as if a tornado or hurricane has blasted through your life and you don't know where the pieces all belong.

Your repair job will require tools, but those tools depend on the damage that was done. You don't need a shop vac if you don't have water damage.

Therefore, your first task in creating an emotional toolbox is to determine what types of tools you may need. You've already done a ton of work on this in the previous discussions and activities.

Focus for a moment on one stressful or difficult situation. What emotion do you associate with that situation? Be more specific than, "I feel good" or "I feel bad". Are you jealous? Disappointed?

Frustrated? Learning to specifically identify your emotions is key in learning how to manage them.

Once you've identified the damage, it's time to determine what types of tools will best serve you in the future. These are tools you will turn to again and again when these or similar situations arise.

These tools can also be called coping mechanisms. Below, you will find a list to get you started. You may find some or all of these tools to be beneficial or they may trigger other ideas for you. This is your toolbox. You will learn what works best for you. It may be that you choose some tools and find they don't work as well as you'd hoped. That's okay. Set them aside and try others.

- Listen to favorite music

- Read a book

- Review pictures that make you happy

- Be creative—draw, color, art journal, and so on

- Breathe deeply

- Practice mindfulness

- Practice gratitude

- Write yourself an uplifting, cheerleader-type of letter to read when you're feeling down

- Have friends write the same type of letter

- Hold ice

- Drink hot tea or another favorite nonalcoholic beverage

- Have a bin of things you can smash

- Work out—even a walk can help

- Have a friend or family member you can call

- Write your feelings down and then tear them up

- Snuggle with a pet

- Use a weighted blanket

- Play music (i.e. a musical instrument)

- Count to 99 by 3's

- Take a nap

- Find something that makes you laugh or smile on YouTube

- Take a bath

- Scream

- Help someone else

- Take a scenic drive

- Hike through nature

Emotional Self-Care Ideas

- Do something that makes you happy

- Practice breathing techniques

- Share only positive posts on social media

- Use adult coloring books or apps

- Be mindful

- Create and recite positive affirmations

- Work toward your goals

- Journal

- Create an inspirational board on Pinterest

- Do something for someone else

- Refrain from judging yourself or being critical

- Do something creative

- Write a letter to someone who has hurt you in the past, then burn it (safely please)

- De-clutter one of the spaces in your home

- Read a book

- Watch a movie you love

- Listen to music you enjoy

- Take a walk in nature—enjoy the scenery

- Go play in the rain
- Relax in a hot bath
- Write five things you're grateful for
- Go play in the park—swing, go down a slide or just be silly
- Write a love letter to yourself
- Give yourself three compliments
- Say no to something you can pass on and yes to you instead
- Enjoy some hot tea
- Buy yourself some flowers
- Enjoy a girls' night with friends who are supportive and positive
- Either go get or give yourself a mani-pedi
- Snuggle up with a favorite pet
- Diffuse some essential oils
- Do a hot wax treatment to your hair or apply a face mask
- Get all dressed up, go out and enjoy a meal at your favorite place
- Create a vision board
- Do a workout—it'll create endorphins
- Do Yoga

Spiritual
Self-Care

Spiritual Self-Care

You don't need to believe in God to practice spiritual self-care. All that is required is to find and nurture a sense of connection to a Higher Power and meaning for your life. Many people don't think much about their spiritual self until they're feeling distressed.

Instead of waiting until you're over the cliff, why not practice spiritual self-care on a regular basis. Who knows, you might even have fewer of those distressing moments.

How you practice spiritual self-care will largely depend on what you believe in. It might include going to services and joining in community with those who share your beliefs. It might mean quiet time and meditation, a time when you can connect to your Higher Power and have some one-on-one time.

Some of the activities you've already read about can also fall under spiritual self-care, like Yoga, mindfulness and meditation.

Cultivating your spiritual life can have several health benefits:

- Optimistic outlook on life
- Greater perceived social support

- Higher resilience to stress

- Lower levels of anxiety

Most spiritual self-care activities help quiet the mind and soothe any turbulence happening behind the scenes.

In this section, there are no worksheets, but instead, a deeper dive into twelve different ways you can practice spiritual self-care. Most of them don't lend themselves to worksheets.

 ## Practice Mindfulness

One of the easiest ways to practice spiritual self-care is to be mindful. Be in the moment, free of anxiety and stress. Notice whatever is around you at that moment. Quiet your mind and be still.

Mindful walking is another way to be mindful, plus it has the added benefit of getting your body moving and your endorphins flowing. As you walk, breathe in the fresh air. Notice the sights and sounds around you. Suspend all judgment and just enjoy where you are.

 ## Try Yoga

Yoga is a practice that seeks to harmonize mind, body and spirit. Many who engage in a Yoga practice gain:

- A sense of inner calm and peace

- The ability to explore the energy surrounding them

- A keener awareness of their surroundings

- A new openness to creativity, healing and overall union

- Knowledge of a physically beneficial way to practice self-care

- The removal of things that may be blocking you from experiencing life fully

The best part about Yoga is that you don't need any equipment. Sure, a mat and a few other standard Yoga accessories might help, but you can do Yoga without any of that.

Meditation

As I mentioned above, meditation comes in a variety of forms. Different religions and spirituality practices use meditation differently. A Christian might read a passage in the Bible and meditate on the meaning in her life while someone who practices Buddhist meditation will use it in an entirely different way.

It doesn't matter what your beliefs are, using meditation can be a great way to feed your spirit. If you don't know where to begin, there are tons of guided meditations on YouTube that will help you.

 ## Gratitude

Boy, we keep coming back to this one, don't we? Well, that should give you some idea as to the many benefits of gratitude! In a relationship, gratitude is a key marker for successful relationships. When you are grateful for your partner and his attributes, it enhances your relationship.

The thing about gratitude is that when you're focusing on what is good in your life, it's tough to put too much energy into the bad.

A practice of gratitude has been shown in many studies to have excellent benefits for your mental and spiritual health, and it's probably one of the easiest things listed in this entire journal.

Commit yourself to writing three different things you're grateful for so you are putting thought and energy into it and not automatically saying, "I'm grateful for my wonderful life." Also, be specific. This helps you really drill down to what's good in your life.

 ## Spend time in nature

This is another repeater, and with good reason! Spending time in nature helps you truly appreciate the beauty of it. Look around you at the vast array of colors. Marvel at how the animals strike a balance among one another.

Enjoy the playfulness of the squirrels as they chase one another up, around and back down the trees. I get foxes and other wildlife in my backyard and I really enjoy looking out to see what they're all up to.

Aside from the sights, spending time in the sunshine provides your body with much-needed vitamin D, and while you can take a vitamin D tablet, the best source is sunshine.

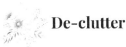 ## De-clutter

I don't know about you, but I reach a point when it's time to de-clutter. I run two successful businesses and sometimes paperwork and other necessary items begin to pile up if I've been particularly busy.

Clutter is distracting and it's an energy suck. Just looking at clutter makes me tired, but clearing it out and looking at a clear space energizes me and helps me be more motivated.

Don't focus on decluttering your whole life at once. Choose a space and start there. As you de-clutter, don't forget to get the human clutter out as well. Human clutter is those negative people in your life. They too are sapping your energy and making you tired.

 ## Find community

All the way back to cavemen, humans have been communal, and we're no different today. Finding community helps you build that support system you need, and it can provide a spiritual backdrop for your life. Many churches and other spiritual groups build themselves around small group communities that focus on specific interests or topics.

Linking up with people who share your beliefs is a great way to develop valuable social links, build your support system and grow intellectually. There are many opportunities to volunteer and show kindness as well. Win-win.

 Journal

Another repeater, journaling is so very beneficial for mind, body and soul. Sometimes the most amazing things come out of what you write in a stream of consciousness. If you truly allow yourself to write without judgment and strictly from whatever your mind sends to your pen, you can learn a lot about what's really lurking in the recesses of your mind.

Take time on a weekly basis to review the entries for the week prior. What themes continue to show up? Are there particular negative thoughts you need to work on? Are certain people showing up? Take note of these things and decide how you can use that review information to have an even better week.

Read books that inspire you

This will be different for everyone. Some authors speak to you in a stronger way than others. Find those authors who seem as if they're speaking to you and then dig in. Ask friends what they like to read.

Look to your community to see what everyone is reading. There may even be a book club you can join or a specific group forming, based on a book or author.

I love to read and I find several authors to be very inspiring, like Dave Hollis (husband to Rachel Hollis of *Girl Wash Your Face* fame) and John Maxwell. You'll find your own authors to follow as you begin to explore.

 Do a technology detox

We are so tethered to technology these days. It seems like we can't go anywhere without our cell phones, which are really mini computers. We must respond to every email, text and phone call right away. Wait—does anyone really call anyone these days?

Turning off technology, even if just for an hour or so, can be really beneficial. The distraction of the constant bing-bongs of alerts is gone. You can focus on your meditation, nature, reading or whatever it is that you're doing to connect spiritually. It can also help you sleep better if you at least turn the noise off.

When you're with others and you're constantly on your phone, it sends a signal to them that they're less important than that email you just got from Zulilly about a shoe sale.

 **Forgive**

Many people hurt us throughout our lives, whether they intend to or not. Instead of forgiving, we tend to hold onto that hurt and allow it to fester and grow. It's like a wound that won't heal.

Often, when I mention forgiveness, someone will tell me that if they forgive, it makes what the other person did to them okay.

This is not what forgiveness is about. You don't even need to tell the person who hurt you that you forgive them.

Forgiveness is for you. It's your way of letting go of the hurt and pain caused by that other person. It's not a way of saying that what happened was okay, it's a way of saying you're not going to let that pain rule your life any longer.

Often when someone has hurt us, we also feel anger or shame. Forgiveness helps to release those emotions, which are not at all productive. They're negatives that need to go away.

If there is someone in your life you need to forgive, whether it's you or someone else, write them a letter of forgiveness. Whether you deliver it or not is up to you. If you don't deliver it, tear it up and throw it away. The act of writing it is what will help you move forward.

 **Treat yourself**

I am a firm believer in treating yourself once in a while. The treat doesn't need to be food, but it can be. It could also be a hot bath with a glass of wine, candles and Netflix playing your favorite series on your iPad while you soak.

Treating yourself is a way of honoring you and acknowledging your self-worth. You do deserve to treat yourself once in a while. You are deserving of love and kindness, especially if you're the one extending it.

This isn't selfish. It's taking time out to appreciate you. You do amazing things every day. Do you recognize that?

Jessica's son, Henri, has severe autism. As a child, Jessica was physically and sexually abused by a man she thought was her father. Every day, Henri is a true challenge. At age 9, he is barely toilet trained, he has limited language skills, he learns visually so he doesn't read or write and he has emotional outbursts typical of someone with his level of autism. Still, Jessica sees herself as worthless because of her abuse. She rarely treats herself to anything and doesn't begin to recognize her amazing and unwavering contributions to this young boy's life.

Unfortunately, Jessica is beyond the coaching I can provide and needs professional help. Still, the many activities in this journal would work well in conjunction with her therapy, if she weren't too ashamed to seek it out.

Intellectual Self-Care

Intellectual Self-Care

I betcha this is a type of self-care you haven't heard much, if anything about. Am I right? What is intellectual self-care anyway?

This type of self-care is all about personal growth. This area of self-care focuses on learning, education and engaging in new activities. Some of the things you've come across in this journal already fall into intellectual self-care, such as reading things that inspire you.

With intellectual self-care, you're nurturing the growth of your mind—your inner thinker. There are several ways in which you can accomplish this. Much like spiritual self-care, there aren't really worksheets to apply here, just concepts and ideas for you to pursue.

Get a library card—and use it

One of the easiest ways to expand your mind is through reading. Before you say you're not a reader, consider trying different types of books.

You don't need to read a 500-page novel. You could check out cookbooks, books on different arts and crafts, books on spirituality or cozy mysteries. Libraries are full of all types of books on dozens of topics. Prowl around and find things that interest you.

You can also get audio books there, if you prefer to listen to books. This is a great way to pass the time when you're exercising or doing something creative.

 ## Find podcasts of interest

There are so many pod-casters out there now that there's no reason to avoid this one. You can find podcasts on any topic, many of them educational. This can help you learn about new hobbies or deepen your spiritual journey.

You can even think of podcasts like old radio shows. Some focus on telling details of history or true crime. Others focus on helping you grow your business, whatever it is, or learning a new skill.

 ## Do puzzles

When I was growing up, we often had a jigsaw puzzle set out somewhere. Dad still works the crossword puzzles in the newspaper and sometimes the Sudoku's or word searches.

Many of these you can get on your phone in a variety of apps. They're great for when you're waiting at the doctor's office or for your kids to come out of school. Puzzles like that stretch your mind and cause you to think outside your normal box. Even if you think you could never finish one, give it a try!

Jigsaw puzzles can also be kind of meditative. It's easy to get lost in finding that one last edge piece or the last orange and red piece to fill in an autumn tree.

You might be thinking that you don't have time for this type of activity, but that's precisely why you should take the time!

Take a class

This one is kind of obvious, but let's expand the definition of class. A class could be a cooking class, a watercolor painting class, an exercise class or a class in how to do CPR.

The point isn't what the class is about but that you're learning something new. Even if you decide at the end of the class that you don't like doing whatever it is you learned, it doesn't matter. It was the learning that was the point.

Aside from that, learning one thing can benefit your life in other ways. For example, I know a few women who make quilts. Learning to do so has helped them learn the value of being precise with measurements and it's helped them with spatial skills as well. Even though you might not like to quilt, you may find that the techniques you learn have value elsewhere.

Change your routine

I love this one for so many reasons! If you're married or dating someone, changing your routine adds a level of mystery that men love.

You don't have to change the whole thing either. Just change one thing, like what coffee you get when you go out together or your route to work. Change how you style your hair, or change the color.

Changing your routine causes your mind to stop and consider this new thing. It's an awakener that is beneficial. How many times have you driven away from your home, only to wonder whether you closed the garage door? Come on, you know you've done it.

But suppose you go the opposite way when you exit your driveway. You're probably going to be more mindful of everything around you because this is new. You'll even notice the garage door.

 ## Join a new group

Meeting up with people who share an interest with you is a great way to grow. Each person brings something new to the table. We all have different life experiences and we come from different places.

Listening to these experiences and seeing the world through someone else's eyes is very educational and interesting.

If you join a group that's focused on a new interest, you're doubling your win by not only learning about the people, but the new topic.

Single-task

Women are notorious for being able to multitask while men often can't. We are single-taskers and we can never figure out how you can have dinner on the table, have your laptop open to your business website and be feeding the baby, all at the same time. And yet, you do it. We admire that but we don't get it.

Try single-tasking. Do just one thing at a time. I know it's a foreign concept but hear me out. If you focus just on cooking dinner, you might come up with new ideas for your recipe. Focusing just on your business for an hour can help you brainstorm past something you've been stuck on for a while.

Slow your roll

You probably spend a great deal of time going 90 miles an hour through life. You need to be at the school by 7:45 to drop off the kids, to work by 8 and to the restaurant to meet your boss for lunch by 11:45. In between, you're stuffing in as much as possible.

Try slowing down. Take the time to breathe and enjoy whatever it is you're working on. Instead of driving while putting on your makeup, talk to your kids and find out what's going on with them at school today.

Take the time to notice people—the barista behind the counter who, now that you look again, seems to have a baby bump and a healthy glow. Notice the elderly couple struggling to get their groceries in the car—can you lend a hand?

Life is going on all around us but we barely take the time to notice. Slow down and check it out.

Social
Self-Care

Social Self-Care

Depending on your personality type, social self-care will either be super-easy for you or it will give you anxiety. I don't want it to give you anxiety, so let's look at how anyone can practice social self-care.

First of all, what is social self-care?

In simplest terms, social self-care is what you do to nurture the relationships in your life. This could be a boyfriend or spouse, a girlfriend, coworkers or family.

If you're a more introverted type of person, you might not have a huge social circle, and that's okay. The definition doesn't say anything about having dozens of people, it just says you're nurturing the relationships you have.

Depending on how your life is currently operating, making time to check in with friends and family might feel a bit challenging. All the more reason to read this section of your self-care journal!

From the very earliest time, humans have been social, communal even. Community is how we look out for one another and protect one another. Any time you see a story on the news about a missing person, especially an elderly person or a child, you see the community rally to search.

After the attacks on 9/11, the United States felt a strong sense of overall community. For a while, people reached out more to their loved ones and spent more time visiting their neighbors.

It's just how we are. We need people. In this section, you will determine what your social self-care needs and find some ideas on how you can practice social self-care.

Nurturing Relationships

The next worksheet is about looking at the relationships in your life to determine which should be nurtured and which should be let go for reasons we've already discussed.

You might only have one or two good friends you can rely upon when you need them. These people should be part of your tool-box and your support system that you learned about earlier.

Again, it isn't the quantity of relationships, it's the quality. And that goes both ways. You should be as good a friend as you're asking them to be. This means sometimes you are the support system.

For some, being the support system is more difficult than being supported and yet, in a truly beneficial relationship, support flows in both directions.

As you grow, physically and emotionally, your friendships may change. Some may fade away while others may grow stronger. As you go through this journal and continue to nurture your own self, you may discover that relationships fade away or become stronger.

It's important to note that friendships left unattended will, like a plant uncared for, wither and die. That's why it's so important to make time in your self-care routine to nurture those relationships.

Some relationships require more at different times. A friend gets married and asks you to be her maid of honor. Your sister has twins and needs help managing her two-year-old in the first few weeks. Someone gets ill, someone close to your friend passes away. Sometimes you're the one going through those experiences.

Kelly's parents have been a real handful lately. She moved in with them a couple of years ago to help care for them but she really didn't think through how it would impact her life until it hit. One morning, her mom collapsed on the floor. Kelly called 911 and the paramedics arrived, hooked her mom up to a bunch of machines and then, all of a sudden, they were getting the paddles out for a defibrillator. Kelly watched in horror as the paramedics set up IV's and hustled her mom out of the house and into the ambulance.

Meanwhile, she heard a text come through on her mom's phone. It was her sister-in-law and she quickly texted her to say that her mom had just left by ambulance with what the paramedics thought was a heart attack. Jeannie, her sister-in-law, called right away and while Kelly's nerves were a mess, talking to Jeannie seemed to help.

Kelly also reached out to her mom's friends in the neighborhood who had certainly seen and heard the ambulance. She asked them to pray for her mom and they also provided a calming effect.

As all this was happening, someone Kelly has worked with for years reached out and she told him what was going on. He too was a voice of calm and reason and helped her to feel even better.

She knew she was fortunate to have a circle of people around her during these challenging emotional moments.

Soon, the hospital called to tell her that her mom hadn't had a heart attack. Kelly and her dad weren't allowed to go because it was during the COVID pandemic, so they were anxiously awaiting any news. She felt terribly relieved and grateful for all the friends she could count on to help her feel better.

Without the relationships Kelly had, she would have struggled through those first few minutes after the event, but because of those relationships, she was able to feel calm and supported. Later, probably because she had sent a prayer request to her church prayer circle, she received an anonymous Blessings Box which contained all kinds of inexpensive but very much appreciated goodies to help Kelly feel better, mind body and soul.

Your social self-care efforts will support the other areas of your self-care routine. In the next worksheet, think through those with whom you feel you have a relationship, weak or strong. Answer the questions and determine where you need to do more nurturing and where you may need to let go, if anywhere.

Deciding on Relationships

When you think back to the last time you really needed a friend, either for a very happy occasion or for a more stressful one. Who did you reach out to?

How did that person respond? Did they offer to jump in and be part of your moment or did they brush you off in lieu of 'something else'? Is this their consistent behavior or is it possible that they truly had something more important to do? Not everyone can be there for you all the time, but they should be able to be there sometimes.

Who is the person who always needs something—$10 for lunch, to borrow your car, someone to cat-sit for a few days—but when you need something, she can't help? She never fills the tank. She forgets to repay the $10.

In which relationships do you always feel as if you're the one who does all the texting, calling, reaching out and so on? Which relationships feel as if you're the only one trying?

Do you have a relationship with anyone who never seems to be able to say nice things about you, your family, your job, your relationships and so on? Friends can offer constructive criticism, and sometimes they see things we don't, but they offer that advice in a kind and loving way. Is there someone who is always putting you down?

Worse than putting you down to your face is the person who speaks negatively about you behind your back. People will talk about you when you're not around, however, if someone truly feels you have a character flaw and they're a true friend, they'll offer it up as that constructive criticism from the prior question. In this instance, the difference is that they won't say it to you, just about you when you're not around.

Think back to the last time something really great happened in your life? Was there anyone who seemed irritated or super-jealous that you experienced that win? Friends should celebrate your wins with you, regardless of whatever crappy thing is going on in their lives (of course, you don't want to rub their noses in it).

The people mentioned in your responses are most likely not true friends or people you should have in your life. I hope there were only one or two names that turned up, but the truth is that when confidence is low, you'll allow anyone into your circle. Now is the time to weed out those who are having a negative influence. If you just cleaned out your entire friend list, don't worry! New friends can be found in your new activities.

Reach Out and Touch Someone

Social self-care isn't all about what someone else can do for you or how others accommodate you. It's also about how you reach out to others and help them when they need it.

When you think about people you consider to be your friends, think about the last time you reached out to them.

Reaching out can also mean helping someone you don't know. I am a big proponent of volunteering somewhere, whether it's a soup kitchen, an animal shelter, a nursing home or with someone you know who needs an extra hand, volunteering is a great way to instantly feel better about yourself!

When you think about reaching out, consider people you know who may be facing a difficult time. It might be a friend who's battling cancer and just needs a warm meal now and then.

It may be an elderly neighbor who needs help with gardening, grocery shopping or shoveling snow.

It could also be a friend with a new baby or someone who is navigating a new life situation, like a divorce or the death of a loved one.

If you aren't paying close attention, it can be easy to miss signs of loneliness, and it plays out in a variety of situations. There are all kinds of ways in which you can reach out and help someone, friend or stranger.

On the next worksheet, you can think through ways in which you can reach out and touch someone with your special gift of kindness and friendliness.

 ## Reaching Out to Someone

1. Plan to Reach Out
First, make a list of your closest friends and family members. Note, at least approximately, if not exactly, when you last reached out to them. Not when you last spoke to them, but when you last reached out. And please don't play the "well I texted her last so it's her turn to text me back" game. It's your turn.

Next, get into your calendar and schedule a time, with reminders, to reach out to that person. Make sure it's within the next week. There's no time like the present!

2. Who do You Know?
In this activity, which you can complete on the next page, think of someone you can help. Think about friends, relatives and neighbors. Think about some individual act of kindness you can do for this person. Here are some ideas:

- Schedule meals to be brought in by other neighbors and/ or friends (there are online tools for this!)

- Offer to run errands or take this person to run their errands

- Offer babysitting, pet sitting or even elderly sitting so this person can get out and enjoy a few moments of 'me time' themselves

- Bake a tasty treat and leave it anonymously on someone's doorstep; challenge them to do the same for someone else

- Give someone a 'Blessings Box' if you know they're going through something challenging; fill it with snacks and self-care items like soap or a candle; leave it anonymously or leave it with your name and contact info, inviting them to reach out if they need a friend

- Offer to help clean someone's house or do some gardening for them Those are just a few ideas. Now, it's your turn.

Here are a few other ways in which you can enrich someone else's day:

- Offer to drive someone to a medical appointment

- Send a quick text to check in and see how someone's day is going—something like, "I was just thinking of you and wishing you a beautiful day"; that might be all they need to feel much better

- Invite someone over for a meal or coffee

- Use skills you have to help someone with a challenging (for them) project; painting, repairing something, creating something unique or teaching them a new skill are great opportunities to spread your craft and help someone in need

- Send a hand-written note on pretty stationery

- Help someone brainstorm through a problem they're having

- Tell someone you haven't spoken to in a while that you miss them

- Share something that made you think of them; "Hey, I heard *Somewhere Over the Rainbow* on the radio the other day and it reminded me of how we used to get together and act out the Wizard of Oz in your back yard"

- Send a humorous meme

- Acknowledge something great they've done, either for you or in general

Social Self-Care Wrap Up

Here are a few more ways in which you can practice social self-care. Mix them up and try to do one each week.

- Invite friends over for a spa night

- Host a game night for you and your friends

- Enjoy a date night with a significant other

- Sneak some cuddles with a furry friend

- Create or join a book club

- Join a home study group from your church

- Invite friends to join you in a progressive dinner where each friend hosts a different portion of the meal

- Take your dog to a dog park and endeavor to meet a new friend

- Join a MeetUp group in your area that focuses their efforts on something you either enjoy now or want to try

- Unite friends in a food drive and donate to a local shelter or church

- Plan a BBQ for friends or family

- Join a recreational sports team

- Just go hang out somewhere public like a coffee shop, a mall or a cozy restaurant; people watch and just enjoy the sights and sounds

- Join a support group if you're battling something difficult

- Leave a funny voicemail for someone

- Mail a surprise care package to someone

Sensory Self-Care

Sensory Self-Care

I know a few young people who suffer from something called Auditory Processing Disorder (APD). I don't mean to begin by bumming you out, but rather to tell you that sensory self-care might not be about introducing things to stimulate your senses. It may be about avoiding too much sensory stimulus.

People with APD can quickly become overwhelmed when there is too much noise, and are then rendered incapable of hearing anything at all.

Another possibility is that you're a highly sensitive person who battles sensory processing sensitivity (SPS). In this instance, you may be often described as shy or introverted. You fall into this category if you:

- Feel you have a rich and complex inner life

- Are deeply moved by art and music

- Can easily become overwhelmed

- Find it difficult to perform a task when someone is watching you

- Are easily startled

- Seem to be oversensitive to pain, caffeine and hunger

- Are very dialed into your inner body sensations

- Notice sensory changes easily—i.e. a new smell or sound

Sensory care activities help you focus on the right sensory experiences for you, the idea being to keep you from feeling overwhelmed. For you, this might mean exposing yourself to a colorful array of flowers or listening to your favorite music. It could also mean turning off the lights, turning off the noise and just sitting in a quiet, dark room.

On the following page are some great sensory self-care ideas for you to try. The best part is that you might be able to combine sensory self-care with any of the other types of self-care for a double-bonus!

 ## Sensory Self-Care Ideas

- Get an adult coloring book and create your own art

- Create different playlists for your different moods

- Get in the garden, get your hands dirty and enjoy either cleaning it up or planting new things

- Sit in a favorite coffee shop and savor the smells

- Open your windows during the next rain or thunderstorm and listen to the weather

- Visit a local museum or arboretum

- Light a candle, turn out the lights and watch the flame flicker

- Find some meditation music and relax

- Go out on a clear evening and do some serious star-gazing

- Take pictures when something catches your eye; scroll through from time to time

- Do nothing—just sit and either enjoy some quiet music or total silence for a few moments

- Find a spot to sit and watch the clouds go by

- Get out and watch a beautiful sunrise or sunset

- Purchase an oil diffuser and try aromatherapy

- Enjoy a favorite treat but really focus on how it tastes

- Get some great-smelling flowers to put on your desk

- Find a fuzzy blanket and just run your fingers through the softness

When you're enjoying sensory self-care, shut everything else out of your mind for a few moments. Be mindful of what you're focused on, whether it's a sight, sound, smell, taste or touch, Just focus on that one sensory input and enjoy it. Don't try to put labels on it. Don't try to over-think it. Just enjoy.

Slowing down to do this can be difficult, but if you take the time, it can also be very refreshing and centering. There's a good chance that taking that type of break can increase your productivity afterward because you've allowed yourself to be quiet, enabling you to refocus your energy.

Self-Care Wrap Up

There is a lot here! Some of the sections are very long compared to others. There is no rush to go through this entire self-care journal. It's more important that you're spending time on yourself than pushing through at an unreasonable pace.

You will likely find some of the activities to be very easy while others may seem insurmountable. If something feels like it's just too difficult, table it for another day.

This is about improving your love for yourself and the amount of time you take to appreciate yourself for who you are.

Self-care is not selfish but necessary if you want to be able to truly take care of those around you who need you. The argument that you just don't have time to take care of yourself because you're busy taking care of others doesn't work.

Avoiding self-care leads you to burnout and feeling over-stimulated. You begin to feel overwhelmed and unable to face anything because it all feels like it's too much.

When you start feeling this way, it's a big cue that you need to step back and practice some self-care.

During the process of learning to take care of yourself, you will begin to feel better about who you are. Your confidence, self-esteem and self-worth will all begin to grow and flourish!

Self-care fits into the Who Holds the Cards Now motto—*Build Yourself and He Will Come.* It's a major building block that many people leave out.

This attracts great men. Whether you have a great man now or you're looking for one doesn't matter. Either way, taking care of yourself should be at the top of your priority list.

Below, you'll find a few links to some things that may help you. Yes, they're products and yes, they cost money, but not much. A few dollars is often the most you'll pay for anything.

Please use this discount code, **SELFCARE**, when shopping in my store. This will get you 25% off your entire order! (Beware, though, it's only good for one use per person so shop well!)

My Books for Women:
who-holds-the-cards-now.myshopify.com/collections/books

Couple's Games:
who-holds-the-cards-now.myshopify.com/
collections/couples-game

For Single Women Only Journals:
who-holds-the-cards-now.myshopify.com/
collections/for-single-girls

Book Bundles:
who-holds-the-cards-now.myshopify.com/
collections/book-bundles

Date Night Kits:
who-holds-the-cards-now.myshopify.com/
collections/date-night-kit

**Also, don't forget to visit my website!
www.whoholdsthecardsnow.com**

Here is the link to The European Journal of Social Psychology mentioned in this book: www.researchgate.net/journal/1099-0992_European_Journal_of_Social_Psychology

Appendix

Journaling

As you've read in the previous sections, journaling is a great way to practice several types of self-care. On the next few pages, you will find some journaling prompts that are well-suited for self-care. Use these when you're stuck for something to write about.

Journaling doesn't need to be very structured. You can do what is called *stream of consciousness* journaling. This means you just sit down and write/type whatever comes to mind. You don't stop to think about it, you just write what comes to you.

This type of journaling can be extremely beneficial if something is bothering you and you need to think it through. Many surprising things come out of stream of consciousness journaling, especially if you truly suspend judgment and analysis of what you're writing.

At other times, you might want to choose a prompt and write about it. There is no right or wrong way to journal. Journaling is for you and you alone. You never have to show it to another living soul.

After you develop the habit of journaling, be sure to look back, once a week or so, and see what types of thoughts and themes are repeating. Is there something particularly negative that keeps coming up, like fear or something making you anxious? Take some time to work through those things.

I read once about a woman who would read through her journaling once a week and look for the repeated use of negative words like "I can't". She would then endeavor to eliminate those words or phrases from her vocabulary. It can be very enlightening to see how many times negativity creeps into our thoughts.

On the next few pages, you will see examples of the journaling pages inside the free workbook. Inside that workbook are many more copies of these pages for you to use.

Don't forget, you can get the workbook at
www.whoholdsthecardsnow.com/
free-self-care-workbook-sign-up/
if you haven't downloaded it already!

Journaling Prompts

- What makes you happy?

- Envision your dream life—what do you see?

- Look ahead five years—what does your life look like?

- What brings you true joy?

- Recall a funny story that makes you laugh out loud every time

- If you could make your living doing anything you wanted to do, what would it be?

- Who is someone you'd like to spend more time with than you do right now?

- What's your favorite physical feature?

- Write your eulogy—what will others say about you after you're gone? Do you want to change this? How?

- Write about the last thing you did that was just for you; how did it make you feel?

- What is one thing you're proud of yourself for?

- What inspires you?

- What is one thing you would like to work on?

- Name something you need to let go of; how will you do this?

- Forgive yourself for something

- Forgive someone else for something

- Recall a favorite memory

- Write about one big thing you're grateful for

- If you could have lunch with one person, alive or not, who would it be and why?

- What does your ideal day look like?

- What thought patterns are keeping you from achieving your goals?

- How are you getting in the way of reaching your full potential?

- What do you need most in order to heal something in your life?

- What makes you a good friend?

- What can you do today to take one step closer to that dream life?

- What makes you feel powerful?

- Have a chat with your teenage self—what advice do you have for her?

- What scares the heck out of you? How can you move past this fear?

- How do you define success?

- What do you think others admire about you?

- Create a list of priorities for the next twelve months

- How can you adjust your morning routine to be more successful?

- How can you honor your body today?

- Write about an important lesson you've learned in the past week

- If you could accomplish one thing in the next three months, what would it be?

- Name something that is totally out of character for you that you'd like to try

- How do you add value to the world?

- What is causing you stress and/or anxiety right now? How can you resolve it?

- What makes you feel calm?

- What makes you feel as if you're in control?

- How can you encourage yourself when you're trying something new?

- What is a choice you made in the last week that was based on your needs?

- Is your current mindset working for you? How can you change it?

- How can you celebrate yourself today?

- What can you do today that you never thought you'd be able to do?

- What is one big goal you'd like to accomplish? Why?

- Write ways in which you can put yourself first without feeling guilty

- Write a letter to yourself, accepting you for who you are

- How can you exchange envy for joy when something great happens to someone else?

- How can you become an advocate for yourself?

- How do you self-soothe?

- How can you make the time you spend with others more intentional?

- Which boundary that you've set or need to set is most challenging? How can you make it less challenging?

- What new opportunities have come out of recent challenges you've faced?

- Remind yourself that you are enough!

- What questions do you want answers for?

- Write about five great accomplishments you've made

- Compare the things you need and the things you want

- Write about your perfect relationship with a man; what does that look like?

- What do you have to offer in a relationship?

- What do you want to save money for? How will you do this?

- How can you make a difference in someone else's life?

- What do you value most?

- How can you help others? Friends or strangers…

- Where would you like to visit? How can you make it happen?

- How can you connect with nature?

- What do you wish your parents would say to you?

- How do you show your generosity?

- How can you be more productive?

- Who could use a surprise gift from you? What will you give them?

- How can you be more organized?

- What would you like to learn?

- Write about your all-time favorite movie

- What would you like to learn from your grandparents?

- What would you do if someone gave you $1000?

- What would you like your child to know about you some day?

- Write ten positive words that describe you

- What coping skills have you developed?

- Write about three decisions you've made that turned out to be awesome

- What expectations do you have of yourself?

- What expectations do others have of you?

- Write about a favorite quote or Bible verse

- What do you want to tell your mother?

- What do you want to tell your father?

- What excuses do you make for yourself?

- Are there things you feel the need to control? How can you let go of that need?

- Who would you like to meet?

- Write about answered prayers

- What is a favorite book? Why?

- What is a task you've been procrastinating? Why? How can you work toward getting it done?

- What are you happy to have done?

- What do you wish you'd never done? Do you need to extend forgiveness to yourself or ask it of someone else?

- Who do you need to forgive?

- Who needs to forgive you?

- What makes you cry?

- What makes you feel better when you're feeling down?

- What is enough to you?

- What do you love about your life?

- What do you want to change about your evening routine?

- What would you like to say no to? How many of those things are you currently doing?

- What would you like to say yes to? How many of those things are you currently doing?

- What are three things that you're doing right now in your life that you need to stop doing? How will you make this happen?

- What is one positive habit you can add to your life?

- How do you recognize that you're approaching burnout?

Journal Page

Gratitude Page

_____

_____

_____

_____

_____

_____

_____

_____

_____

_____

_____

_____

_____

_____

_____

_____

_____

_____

_____

_____

_____

_____

_____

The Year of Me: Year _____

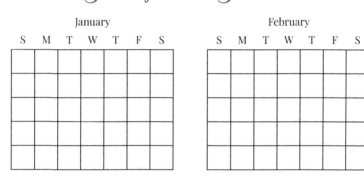

January

S	M	T	W	T	F	S

February

S	M	T	W	T	F	S

May

S	M	T	W	T	F	S

June

S	M	T	W	T	F	S

September

S	M	T	W	T	F	S

October

S	M	T	W	T	F	S

Notes

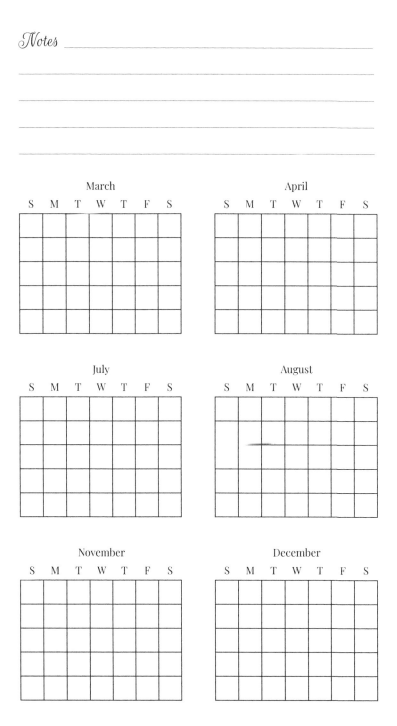

March

S	M	T	W	T	F	S

April

S	M	T	W	T	F	S

July

S	M	T	W	T	F	S

August

S	M	T	W	T	F	S

November

S	M	T	W	T	F	S

December

S	M	T	W	T	F	S

What's Going On for the Next Twelve Months?

MONTH: _____

MONTH: _____

MONTH: _____

MONTH: _____

MONTH: _____

MONTH: _____

What's Going On for the Next Twelve Months?

MONTH: _____

MONTH: _____

MONTH: _____

MONTH: _____

MONTH: _____

MONTH: _____

What's Going On This Month: _____

1 _____
2 _____
3 _____
4 _____
5 _____
6 _____
7 _____
8 _____
9 _____
10 _____
11 _____
12 _____
13 _____
14 _____
15 _____
16 _____
17 _____
18 _____
19 _____
20 _____
21 _____
22 _____
23 _____
24 _____
25 _____
26 _____
27 _____
28 _____
29 _____
30 _____
31 _____

Month

Sunday	Monday	Tuesday	Wednesday	Thursday	Friday	Saturday

This Week: _____

MONTH:

S	M	T	W	T	F	S

This Week's Self-Care Includes:

_____
_____
_____
_____

MONDAY	TUESDAY	WEDNESDAY

This Week's Goals:

_____
_____
_____
_____

Goal Associated Tasks:

_____
_____
_____
_____

This Week's Top 5:

_____
_____
_____
_____
_____

THURSDAY	FRIDAY	SATURDAY/SUNDAY

Notes:

_____
_____
_____
_____

Today is: _____

Today's Top 3:
_____
_____
_____
_____
_____

6:00 _____
6:30 _____
7:00 _____
7:30 _____
8:00 _____
8:30 _____
9:00 _____
9:30 _____
10:00 _____
10:30 _____
11:00 _____
11:30 _____
12:00 _____
12:30 _____
1:00 _____
1:30 _____
2:00 _____
2:30 _____
3:00 _____
3:30 _____
4:00 _____
4:30 _____
5:00 _____
5:30 _____
6:00 _____
6:30 _____
7:00 _____
7:30 _____
8:00 _____
8:30 _____
9:00 _____

Twelve Months of Healthy Challenges

Below, you have twelve boxes in which you can write 12 different healthy challenges to try. I've given you a few ideas below, but feel free to brainstorm your own.

- 3 Servings of veggies a day
- Workout X times a week (you pick the number)
- X steps per day—a great way to compete with one another!
- No soda challenge
- X Ounces of water challenge (shoot for 1/2 your body weight in ounces; ex: 150 lbs=75 oz)
- No sugar challenges
- No fast food/eating out challenge
- Walk or bike where you can for the month
- Protein shakes once a day
- No cheat days challenge
- Focus on a particular exercise (squats, burpees, running, walking, & so on)
- Meal plan an entire month and stick to it!

1	2	3	4
5	6	7	8
9	10	11	12

Made in the USA
Middletown, DE
01 October 2023

39916331R00106